COMPETITION TROUT FISHING

COMPETITION
TROUT FISHING

CHRIS OGBORNE

The Crowood Press

First published in 1988 by
The Crowood Press
Ramsbury, Marlborough,
Wiltshire SN8 2HE

British Library Cataloguing in Publication Data
Ogborne, Chris
    Competition trout fishing.
    1.   Trout. Fly fishing
    I.   Title
    799.1'755

ISBN 1 85223 043 6

Typeset by Inforum Ltd, Portsmouth
Printed in Great Britain by Butler & Tanner Ltd, Frome and London

Contents

Acknowledgements

I should like to express my sincere thanks to Sandy Leventon, Editor of *Trout & Salmon* magazine, and to Chris Dawn of *Trout Fisherman* magazine for allowing me to use extracts from articles originally written for them.

Special thanks also to that great man of our sport, Tony Pawson. Not only has he been a constant source of help and encouragement, but he has allowed me to use some of the historical data featured in his excellent book, *Competitive Fly Fishing*.

Peter Gathercole's brilliant photography appears throughout the pages of this book, and it seems that Peter is always on hand to record the best moments of every major competition. Some of his shots appear here by kind permission of Benson & Hedges, who first commissioned them. Indeed, I should like to record my gratitude, and that of my fellow anglers, to Benson & Hedges, who have done so much to elevate the status of competition fly fishing.

A very special thank you to one fellow competitor who has made a major contribution to this work, my good friend Peter Thomas. Peter is one of the best known and most able anglers in the field and his specialist knowledge of Mask has been invaluable.

And finally, my thanks to all the boat partners and fellow anglers, with whom I have shared so much over the years. Fishermen are a special breed of people, and life is that much richer for happy memories of days on the water.

Foreword

Following the boom in reservoir and still-water fishing there has been a great surge of interest in competitive fly fishing. Such competition has a long and honourable tradition in Britain, but until recently it was only in Scotland that it was a major part of the fly fishing scene. Now in the rest of Britain ever-growing numbers are becoming sold on its attractions, having sampled its delights and despairs, its friendships and its unique opportunities for learning. Typical of recent converts is that entertaining fishing writer and expert nymph and floating line fisherman, Jeremy Lucas. After many years holding the view that competition was not an appropriate part of fishing he was persuaded to give it a try; he wrote to me at the end of 1987, 'What a wonderful season it has been. It was my first in competition and I am totally hooked. I wish I had gone into it earlier.'

No doubt winning the European Open at Bewl, and being a member of a team which so nearly won the Benson & Hedges that year was a decisive factor in changing Jeremy's attitude. But his response reflects the experience of so many fishermen who put aside doubts, give it a go, and find out what an enthralling experience competition trout fishing can be. Who better to outline its attractions and give advice on every aspect of the sport than Chris Ogborne? Since you are about to have the pleasure of reading his book there is no need for me to emphasise what a lucid and

interesting writer he is, how original in thought, and how easy to follow in his advice on complex matters. Because he is as modest as he is expert it may not be so immediately apparent what an outstanding fisherman he is. My first day out with Chris was on his home water of Blagdon, the original and still the most attractive of our 'reservoirs', about which Chris himself has written the definitive book. It was a sunny day at the season's end, with only educated and difficult fish left. My leisurely hours were spent watching Chris net trout, and admiring his skill. When I fished normally I only moved the occasional one. When I fished as fine as Chris I got broken. At once it was clear to me that whilst I might have won a world championship river fishing, I was nowhere near his league as a stillwater or reservoir angler. And Chris is just as good on rivers!

One of the values of competition fishing is that it soon shows whether a reputation is deserved or spurious. So many of those 'pundits' who pontificate to us about the right way to fish (which usually amounts only to an account of their personal preferences and prejudices) are mere spinners of phrases and pickers of brains. All the more credit then to those like Chris, or Bob Church, or Jeremy Lucas, who are prepared to come down from the safe heights of 'authoritative' writing and keep proving their genuine ability in competition with the rest of us. There is, of course, much more to fishing than catching fish, as the 'only here for the scenery' writers continually remind us. But the *skills* of fishing are about trying to outwit and catch the fish; these skills are only truly proven in competition.

One myth which competition quickly dispels is that catching fish is as much a matter of luck as skill. Luck *is* a significant factor, enough to add spice to competitive fishing so that on a 'lucky' day the average performer may see off the expert. In that regard it is like bridge in that if just one rubber is played a couple of novices may defeat Rixi Marcus and Terence Rees; but over ten rubbers the novices will be beaten out of sight. The 1987 World Fly Fishing Championship in England illustrated clearly that consistently good results depend on skill rather than chance. With at least a hundred expert anglers from over twenty countries involved in this week-long event, the favourites were Brian Leadbetter and Chris Ogborne. Not surprisingly Brian and Chris, who had continually proved themselves outstanding in competition, came in first and second respectively. Chris rubbed it in by winning the National final (again!), qualifying for both Home Internationals (both won by England), and winning the Brown Bowl as best rod in the Autumn International on Leven. Having won the World Championship, Brian won the European Open at Weiswampach for the second successive year and, with John Pawson, was a member of the winning teams in both European Opens in France and Belgium, and of the 'World Cup' team event. England won the World Cup with more than double the points of the runners-up, Australia, and more than triple those of third-placed New Zealand! Chris, incidentally, hasn't yet been able to fit in coming to one of Europe's Opens, which has given the rest of us a chance!

The year 1987 certainly underlined the skill and consistency which has made Chris, and Brian Leadbetter, unquestionably the best all-round fly fishermen of the moment; their surplus of skill totally nullified the 'luck' factor. Both are also outstanding team men, who will pass on all their knowledge to the other members. Chris mentions the remarkable spirit in the England World Fly Fishing Championship team, and that even in the individual event they were exchanging flies and advice even though they were in direct competition for the top individual places. What he doesn't mention is that it was Chris himself, who, having fished brilliantly at Avington the day before, was up at six o'clock on the final morning tying more of his special patterns in case these might help Brian Leadbetter or my son John. Friendship could go no further since that might well have affected his placing or even cost him the title for all he then knew. In that same spirit, the spirit which makes most fly fishing competitions such happy occasions, he passes on here all the methods and ideas which have made him such an outstanding champion.

There is only one thing Chris can't pass on; that is the 'X' factor of competition fishing, the special 'feel' some have for choosing the right method, the right fly for the moment, when there is such a range of possibility. In seven hours' fishing in the world championship session on Rutland Brian Leadbetter caught steadily all the time, but only because he made seven changes of line and got it right each time. How many of us would have just kept pegging away with the line that was successful at the start and missed out on the remarkable catches that he and my son had on that memorable day? I once asked Bob Draper, for so long the outstanding reservoir angler and England captain, for his view of this 'X' factor. 'It's like a gardener with green fingers. Either you have it, or acquire it by personal experience, or you don't. No one can teach it.'

Every other secret of Chris's phenomenal success is set out in this book for you. Only you can add that 'X' factor. As the comedians say, it's not just the jokes, it's the way you tell them. Here Chris tells all there is to know about competition trout fishing. The rest is up to you, but you cannot fail to benefit in some way from his advice, which is as relevant to ordinary fishing as it is to competition.

Tony Pawson

Preface

Twentieth-century life is competitive. Village fishermen in the far-flung corners of Britain compete with Nature to extract a living from the sea. Young executives in an increasingly business-orientated world compete with each other to climb the ladder of success. And sadly, in some areas, people compete for the very job that earns them their living.

Competition, in all its forms, is an established fact of life. Indeed, as a nation of some considerable sporting prowess, Britain takes pride in its achievements in many fields. Some of the most successful television programmes have revolved around a quiz, tournament, or quasi-sporting event. Each year, the nation becomes preoccupied with Wimbledon, Wembley or Silverstone. And recently, even those who should be in their beds by midnight have burned many a gallon of night oil as the likes of Davis and Thorburn

Well-found boats, clean water, and a good wave. This is Lough Melvin.

have locked horns over a green baize rectangle. The plain truth is that the vast majority of us enjoy competitions, however minor and in whatever form.

This enjoyment is in no way diminished if the sport in question happens to be of a peaceful or sedentary nature, although those adjectives do not always apply to fly fishing. It is an oft-quoted statistic that fishing is the largest participant sport in the UK, with upwards of four million anglers seeking the pleasures of rod and line every week. Within that vast band of people lies a total cross-section of society: Lords and MPs rub shoulders with farmhands and sales representatives, finding in fishing a common language of communication, and a subject that they can discuss on equal terms. I was once fishing a small moorland stream in Devon, and was in discussion with the water bailiff. As we talked, two anglers approached on the far bank. The bailiff quietly informed me that one was a Colonel, and the other an out-of-work miner. From their animated conversation, it was obvious that a new friendship was being forged. But what was impossible to tell, was which one was the Colonel and which one the miner.

At the very outset of this book perhaps we should define the word 'sport' in terms of its application to fly fishing. I firmly believe, as do thousands of anglers, that fishing is a sport first and a recreation second. The popular conception of an angler is someone who sits interminably

'Entente cordiale'. Anglers from three nations discuss tactics.

under a large green umbrella, and whose only activity is confined to re-casting his float on to the water, every hour, on the hour. Devotees of fly fishing, however, will know just how much energy is expended during a day on the water, with many of us arriving home late in the evening in a state of near exhaustion, often needing a full day's rest to recover from this 'peaceful pastime'.

Statistics, thankfully, have little to do with fly fishing. It is difficult to say just how great a proportion of our four million general anglers take to the fly rod. What is beyond doubt, though, is that the number is increasing, and increasing very rapidly. The proliferation of inland stillwater fisheries in recent years has meant that fly fishing is within easy reach of most, and is available at a price that is in no way prohibitive.

I also firmly believe that the numerical growth is due in no small measure to the increased interest in fly fishing competitions. As recently as ten years ago, scant attention was paid to the Internationals, twice-yearly confrontations between the four Home Nations (England, Scotland, Wales and Ireland). Yet now, in England alone, over two thousand anglers compete for a coveted place in the annual squad, and the National final is the piscatorial equivalent of the football Cup Final. Other major tournaments have also contributed. The Benson & Hedges annual team competition has brought international fishing to local club level, and their sponsorship is sufficiently generous that no individual need be reluctant to enter on grounds of expense. It is truly the 'Everyman's International'.

Surely every thinking angler must welcome these developments in our sport, for all the major competitions seek only to promote that which is good, traditional, and ethical in fly fishing. International rules, which are defined and discussed later in this book, reflect the very essence of 'loch style', a way of fishing that has evolved over generations of loch and lough fishermen in Scotland and Ireland. Along with the sport, the rules themselves have evolved, and as far as possible they eliminate the luck factor, thus allowing skill to win through.

But the smallest rule is undoubtedly the most important: at the bottom of most rule sheets it simply states 'please observe the courtesies of the boat'. In simple terms this means that each angler should have a regard for his fellow. At the start of a competition day two fishermen, who may never have seen each other before, will take to the water together. If they observe the basic courtesies they will part at the end of the day having shared good sport and good company. But if they read further into the rule, and share ideas or flies, perhaps a dram, and maybe help each other to net a fish or tie a new leader configuration, then they will part in the evening as *friends*, with an arrangement to share another boat at some time in the future.

This is really what competitive fly fishing is all about, a far cry from the tooth and nail affair that some journalists would have you believe. Neither is it anything to do with glum faces and despair at empty creels. Rather, it is a vehicle for anglers from all walks of life to share excitement, expectation, and friendship.

Competitive fly fishing is also a platform for the development of new ideas, techniques and methods. Few things improve by standing still, and fly fishing must con-

Nick Nicholson – obviously happy about something.

tinue to evolve for the safety of its future. Innovations that are pioneered in the competitive field quickly become established as standard techniques, as those of greater ability share their findings with the rest of us.

This book is a humble attempt by one committed and dedicated competition fly fisherman to paint a picture of the scene as it is today. I will try to share some thoughts and theories of my own, as well as drawing on the experience of the many fellow competitors who I have been privileged to know over the years. For the newcomer to the sport I will try to weave a path through the potential minefield of tackle and technique. If I can encourage just one new angler to enter this fantastic branch of angling, then this book will have been a success.

1 A Brief History

Humble Beginnings

Given the nature of humankind, it is impossible to say when the first fly fishing competition took place. Whenever two or more anglers go fishing together, there is an element of competition – no matter how carefully it is concealed. There is very little that can genuinely be termed new in our sport. As we shall see later an awful lot of fly patterns are really only variations on an established theme, and it is a sobering experience to read through a first edition of some angling treatise by a past master and discover that a minor nymph tactic was developed several hundred years ago – just when you thought you had 'discovered' it for yourself.

I also feel it is not particularly relevant to list all those early encounters that are so often referred to as the beginning of fly fishing competition. They have all been documented before, and in the main they make yawningly boring reading. However, I have always believed in giving credit where due, and it is probably because of some extremely far-sighted thinking in the early days that the development of competition fishing has followed the path that has led to its present-day status. As a consequence, it is only fair to set the record straight with some particularly noteworthy dates.

The birth of competitive loch style fishing probably took place in the early nineteenth century. In those days, the results of competitions were of local interest only, and as such were scantily recorded. Very little information exists about the many Scottish club competitions that must have taken place, and in the main they seem to have been fairly friendly, parochial affairs. What is certain, though, is that everyone had a preference for one principal venue – Loch Leven. Then, as now, Leven was supreme as a base for loch style fishing, and its great size, prolific insect life, and great head of natural wild brown trout have been legendary for many generations.

So from relatively humble beginnings of inter-club, inter-personal competition, the groundswell of popularity was moving towards something more formal, and more substantial. Just as they do today these early anglers realised that the existence of competitive fly fishing provided them with an open forum for ideas, and a sounding board for new techniques. If such an event could be coupled with an excuse for a few days in convivial and like-minded company, along with a dram or two, then so much the better. In that respect at least, little has changed.

Loch Style Origins

The inaugural Scottish National, so often referred to as the start of competitive loch style fishing, took place on Loch Leven on 1 July 1880. Yet it was by no means the first of its kind. Leven records show that in 1873 no less than 26 different club competitions took place, with some 463 anglers competing. No doubt this initial level of popularity prompted the organisers to look at the possibility of a more serious event.

At that first event in 1880 Peter Malloch (Malloch of Perth, the tackle maker) took the heaviest fish. The entry was restricted to 32 names, although in effect it was over-subscribed many times. Right through the turn of the century this Scottish National event took place annually. Although on occasions there were visiting teams participating on a 'friendly' basis, it was essentially a Scottish affair, always taking place on Leven.

There are several myths that need to be dispelled at this stage. Firstly, Leven did *not* always fish well in the 'good old days'. Just as in modern times, it seems that Leven was a loch that had its ups and downs, with brilliantly good years mixed with dour and unproductive seasons. Nevertheless, such was its appeal that Leven, being one of only very few still waters in existence, pulled in anglers from all over Britain, mostly because there was nowhere else to go. It was not until 1904 that Blagdon opened for business as one of the very first stillwater fisheries in England.

The second myth to bite the dust is the popularly-held belief that taking big bags of fish in a competition day is only a modern problem. Many of today's competitors are branded as 'stockie bashers', or something of a similar derogatory nature. Consider, then, our friend Peter Malloch of Perth, who in the Leven National of 1912 took no less than 37 fish. By the strangest coincidence that is exactly the number of

trout taken by Brian Leadbetter at Rutland, in the 1987 World Fly Fishing Championships. Again, history has a pleasant habit of repeating itself!

The English have never been slow to cotton on to a good thing north of the Border – smoked salmon and Scotch whisky to name but two – and it was in many ways inevitable that the northern-based English clubs should have looked with some envy at this annual Leven jamboree. So in May of 1928 the English International Fly Fishing Association was formed, with the specific intent of fielding a team against the Scots. Thus in 1928 the first true International was fished, with teams of 20 competing on Leven. The English team included such celebrities as J.J. Hardy (another tackle maker) and was due to have been captained by H.R.H. the Duke of York. Regrettably, affairs of state precluded the latter from taking part, but his nomination at least ensured a very considerable interest among the general angling public.

Only four years elapsed before the rest of the Home Nations decided to get in on the act, and in 1932 the first International between England, Scotland, Ireland and Wales was fished. Because of the pressure on the number of boats on Leven, teams were then 16 strong. In all other respects, the competition mirrored very closely the ones that we enjoy today, save some important technical differences. Firstly there was only one full International each year, and secondly the selection process was a very different affair.

These Internationals continued unchanged for many decades, the only break being during the Second World War. However, 1950 saw some fundamental changes take place, and the 1970s especial-

15

ly was a period of inspired thought on the part of many people.

Until 1971, although there had been only one formal Spring International in each calendar year, there were also the autumn friendly matches. With all the Home Nations now competing, and with a relatively high level of expense for all visiting teams to Leven, it was only fair that a system of rotating the venue should be introduced, with all four countries selecting a venue every second year. Thus there were now two Internationals in a calendar year, and competitors had the chance to broaden their horizons. The first venue chosen, Lough Lein in Killarney, was such a success that a very happy seal of approval was given.

Not so happy, though, in the English camp. The Scots and Irish had long pioneered the democratic process of team selection, whereby an angler qualified by *performance*. England and Wales were much slower in this respect, preferring to choose team members by *reputation*. Things came to a head in 1972, and after a series of altercations the English IFFA withdrew from all Internationals, thus leaving England unrepresented for three matches.

With the marvellous spirit that now pervades every competition it is hard to believe that feelings could have been allowed to run so high. However, with the benefit of hindsight, many of the protagonists now agree that it was probably time for a change, and it is certain that the system now operating in England would be hard to fault. Just to set the record straight, most of the people involved in the upset have long since buried their hatchets, and are now the best of friends. They even have an annual 'fun match' between

the old Federation and the new Confederation, so common sense and angling spirit appear to have won through in the end!

In 1974, the Confederation of English Fly Fishers (CEFF) was formed, and England re-entered the International series that autumn at Trawsfynydd. Their team selection procedure remains to this day, and is a model for all. There are regional heats through all the local Federations that make up the Confederation, culminating in a national final to select the two teams for the coming year.

The last date in this short chronology is a happy one indeed. In 1982 the Internationals celebrated their jubilee year with the spring competition on Trawsfynydd. It is a particularly poignant memory for me, as this was my first-ever International, having qualified to fish for England by winning the National at Rutland in 1981. Obviously, the jubilee year made it a very special occasion, and one that will linger long in my memory.

Other Traditions

When looking at the history of competitive fly fishing it is all too easy to become preoccupied with the National and International series. Without a doubt they deserve great prominence, acting as they did as a starting point for all the rest, but they were by no means alone in the field.

It is worth noting that the huge variety of stillwater fishing we currently enjoy is, in fact, a fairly modern phenomenon. In the last thirty years demand for supply water in England has been such that many new reservoirs have been formed, most of which have been prepared to open their doors to the angling fraternity. Before this

Pretending to be calm, just before the gun.

time it was the natural Lochs and Loughs that provided the sport, and most of these were to be found in Scotland and Ireland.

Fishing in Ireland is not so much a sport as a way of life, with a huge number of people involved. The vastness of loughs such as Mask and Conn means that a ghillie is more or less obligatory, not just to find the fish but also to navigate in safety. As a consequence, a complete folklore has built up around the Irish ghillies, and their angling prowess is legendary. Couple this with the obvious commercial advantages of a tourist industry, a green and pleasant landscape, and the natural friendliness of the natives, and it is small wonder that countless generations have made their way across the Irish Sea in search of trout.

The modern 'International' on Lough Melvin, which is only a decade old, was preceeded in 1937 by a match between England and Ireland, of a very friendly nature. But the canny Irish wanted something more substantial and, particularly, they wanted an event that would bring many more than just three teams of 16 rods to their shores. Consequently, in 1964 the first Lough Conn Intercontinental competition was held. This remains today as a big prize money event, with the accent more on individual than on team performance. It covers three full days, and is superb in every way. Four-figure prize money attracts anglers from all over Europe, and extra sponsorship from local traders ensures a full prize list. Now

17

known as the Crossmolina Angling Festival, it is an annual event not to be missed.

In a similar vein, though in many people's eyes even more prestigious, is the Lough Mask 'World Cup', which has been fished each year since 1965. Mask is a limestone lough, situated in County Mayo, and is a serious challenge for any fly fisherman. The formal title of the event is the World Open Wet-Fly Fishing Championship, but everyone refers to it as the 'World Cup' – although there is some danger in this being confused with the World Fly Fishing Championship (WFFC), which is another thing entirely.

The really great thing about loch style competition in Ireland is the absolute sense of tradition. Not for them the 'new-fangled' ideas that have emerged in recent years from the English stillwater scene. You will not see anyone on Lough Melvin employing Northampton style from the back of the boat, and rarely will they indulge in the long-lining Bristol style, so successful on Chew, Rutland, or Grafham. No, the Irish stick to their traditional short lines, with teams of three or four wet flies that have withstood all the tests of time.

As such, their contribution to the continuity of competitive fly fishing history is immense and invaluable.

Finally, perhaps the greatest competition of them all is the World Fly Fishing Championship, held under the truly international auspices of Confederation Internationale de la Peche Sportive (CIPS). First held in Luxemburg in 1981, the WFFC was regarded by many as having genuinely come of age in 1987 when England was the host nation. No less than 21 nations sent teams of six anglers to test their skills at venues as diverse as Rutland, Grafham, Avington and the River Test. The rest is history, and is well documented elsewhere in this book. Suffice to say for the moment that the many links and intercontinental friendships that were formed during May 1987 will surely make fly fishing much richer.

From those early days in 1880, right through to modern competitive fly fishing, the basic Olympian ideal of man talking to man, and nation to nation, has been at the centre of every event. If anglers hold true to this ideal, the future of our sport is assured.

2 Competitions Today

Club, Regional and Local

There has been a huge growth in interest in competitive fly fishing in the last decade. The International format in Scotland, where it originally began, grew basically from a strong club scene. In England, Wales and Ireland it was largely the other way around, in that the major competitions prompted more interest at local and club level.

Most of the real growth took place in the early and mid-1980s, a period that saw the proliferation of regional tournaments, no doubt prompted by the apparent glamour of the International scene. Small local clubs and associations found themselves pressurised by their membership to hold their own annual competitions, which often proved to be great social events – a tangible bonus. So the scene at club level is currently prospering as never before.

As in so many sports, *real* developments take place by virtue of the fact that successful anglers develop new methods and techniques, and these in turn are passed on to fellow fishermen. In local competitions lesser anglers can learn and improve by watching others who are more competent. Happily, the opposite is also true. Nobody has all the answers, and even the acknowledged experts will freely admit that they are always learning. An angler of many years' competition experience may find that he can learn from a new beginner who has unwittingly stumbled upon an effective nuance of tactic. This again is the essence of club competition, and indeed of competitions in general. The easy, friendly atmosphere makes an ideal breeding ground for new friendships and new ideas.

Local sponsorship is another benefit of the increased interest in competitions. Whilst most people are aware of the obvious exposure that is gained from a major national event so too are local companies seeking to sponsor local clubs. My own club, the Bristol Reservoirs FFA, has enjoyed sponsorship in the last four years from a paint manufacturer, a sherry company and an estate agency. All have been more than pleased with the exposure that they have received and have regarded the sponsorship as an investment in the future.

It is at local level too that many anglers begin the long trek towards the distant goal of representing their country. Most regional federations are involved in their own pre-qualifying matches for the National finals, and many of them are run under club auspices. Success at local level can sow the seed of ambition in many a young angler, and this is a driving force that most clubs are happy to encourage. Again in Bristol we have a winter programme which positively helps youngsters through the mystique of fly tying and casting, in the hope that somewhere in the sea of eager faces there may be a national champion in the making.

Bristol Reservoirs FFA. One of the most successful club teams of all time.

Internationals

International competition has developed from relatively humble beginnings into a fully-fledged Home International event. It is to the eternal credit of all involved that it has done so with virtually no major funding, preferring instead to retain the genuine amateur status of a true sporting tradition.

There is no experience quite like fishing for your country, but you must make a commitment some fifteen months, or more, in advance. In spring you enter your local federation's system of pre-qualifiers, which in busy areas like the Midlands can involve you in upwards of three competitions. Assuming that you are successful here you move on to the National final. This is a major achievement in itself, because you may be faced with odds of one in twenty at regional level – figures that leave precious little margin for error!

The National final, in England at least, usually takes place in September. Depending on the size of the chosen venue there

Bristol's John Braithwaite says 'two fish'.

will be some sixty to eighty anglers, competing for the coveted top twenty places. At each International the top four rods of each team qualify automatically on merit for the next year's series. The top ten places in the National final go to the Spring International in the following year, whilst the second ten join the Autumn team, thus giving the full team of fourteen anglers. Variations on this theme operate in all the Home Countries, but in essence the principle is the same, if not the timetable.

It can be seen that, in England at least, an angler is faced with a long haul. He may register for an eliminator in February of one year, and find himself qualifying for a September International in the following year. It is a long wait, but what an experience it is! At the end of the National, with the nail-biting worry at the weigh-in, the delay before results are announced seems interminable. But then when your name *is* on the list the full realisation sinks in. You will actually be 'doing your bit' for your country next year!

Even then, there is a kind of surreal quality about waiting for your full International place. Many anglers of my acquaintance have said that they don't know when the reality of their 'cap' truly sinks in. Some say it is a few days before the match, when they are presented with their blazer badges to be sewn on before

21

the International dinner. Others say it is when the England captain enacts the delightful tradition of pinning a red rose to your jacket on the morning of match day. And yet others that it is the walk to the boats, as a team, that provides the final realisation. As ever, and as in everything about fishing, it is an individual and a personal thing.

It is also something that never pales, no matter how many times you represent your country. After many years of competitive fly fishing I generally reckon to have overcome the proverbial pre-match nerves, and can feel fairly relaxed about the preparations. Not so with an International. Somehow, the very fact that you *are* representing your country gives an added stigma, and control of adrenalin simply slips away!

This is never more true than when you are given what is perhaps the ultimate honour, that of captaincy of the National squad. This was a privilege I enjoyed in 1986, in the Spring International at Trawsfynydd. It is very much a mental balancing

Near-exhaustion at the end of eight hours afloat.

act to try to encourage newcomers to the team, coolly discuss tactics with old stagers, and try to appear both confident and nonchalant at the same time. Very few can achieve the balance – and I will be the first to say that I am not one of them!

The International scene has never been in better shape than it is today. Largely, the International Fly Fishing Association administers the events efficiently, and with a benevolent hand. From the competitor's viewpoint the twice-yearly competitions are conducted in the best possible spirit, and with the minimum of reference to 'the rules'. I do not propose to itemise all the IFFA rules for precisely the same reason that I avoided cataloguing the sport's historical intricacies – they are horrifically boring. Thankfully they are also mostly unnecessary, as competitors are generally fully aware of the common-sense rules that govern loch style fishing. Ninety per cent of the rules catalogue can be summarised by the following simple paragraph.

International loch style competition involves two anglers and a boatman to each boat. Boats drift freely downwind, unless conditions dictate that a drogue may be used. Each angler fishes his 'half' of the boat, using flies of a prescribed size and almost any conventional line. If each angler observes the courtesies of the boat, all is well.

Nothing could be simpler than this basis, on which all competitions are fished. The real *esprit de corps* of fly fishing competition dictates that we need a minimum rather than a maximum number of rules; the absurdities that arise by too close a scrutiny of every rule are clear evidence of this. Of course everyone should be brought down to a common

The Welsh daffodil is worn with pride at an IFFA match.

starting point, as this will allow skill rather than luck to come to the fore, but the over-enthusiastic application of minor restrictions is not something most fly fishing competitors appreciate or value.

Broadly speaking, England is in good order on the International scene. Major sponsorship is discreet, as indeed it was intended to be, but many competitors have benefited from generous sponsorship which has ensured that no angler is precluded from representing his country by virtue of his financial status. It is to be hoped that similar support will continue.

However, to be realistic and fair it should also be stated that not all anglers agree with the amateur philosophy, and many would welcome the introduction of big money sponsorship, reported to be 'just around the corner'. Personally I feel that

Dennis Buck, Brian Leadbetter and John Pawson.

this might be to the detriment of the sport in some ways, but not all. There is, and must always be, room for compromise.

Fly fishing is intrinsically a gentle art and, despite the excitement and enjoyment of competitions, it is essentially a solitary contest between man and fish. If large sums of money were hanging on the reaction of one trout to a fly, I fear that some of the genuine sentiment may be lost.

Bank Competitions

I have restricted the subject matter of this book almost exclusively to boat fishing largely because every major fly fishing competition is conducted in loch style format from boats, with bank competitions being something of a rarity. Another reason for leaving the subject of bank competitions well alone is that they demand a totally different set of tackle, tactics, and technique. So much so, in fact, that this would warrant a separate book in its own right. By their nature, bank competitions

24

are difficult to control, and the organisers have to rely on the integrity of the participants in terms of sticking to the rules. When a local club element is involved, and where everyone knows everyone else, this is obviously less of a problem.

At present bank competitions tend to be local affairs, organised at club level. The only exception to this is the occasional blending of boat and bank fishing that takes place in events like the World Fly Fishing Championship, which adds an extra dimension of interest. But for the most part the major events are essentially loch style competitions, and they command the most attention.

This is not meant to denigrate bank fishing in any way at all, as there is an equal amount of skill in both arms of the sport. Indeed in some ways there can be a greater demand on the bank angler's ability to read the water, as he must be prepared to accept a designated 'swim', or small section of bankside, and has to exploit all of its possibilities. Not for him the expanse of the lake in which to drift; rather, he is tied down by the draw, and has to make the best of things whatever wind and wave throw at him. Even if he is given the freedom to walk the bank and to select his own spot, he still needs to find the fish for himself and to ascertain the effective tactics for catching them. He does not have the companionship of a boat partner that we enjoy in loch style, and can feel positively 'out on a limb' at times.

In my opinion there is a strong case for exploiting the possibilities of bank competitions, if for no other reason than they lend themselves ideally to a format for spectators. Venues like Avington, Dever Springs, Damerham or Kingfisher would all be able to offer facilities to those who might care to watch expert anglers at work, and there is little doubt that many would take advantage of this. Similarly, sponsors might enjoy the chance to entertain visitors.

Just as boat fishing tactics can be markedly different on Chew or Leven, so too can they vary when bank fishing on places as diverse as Rockbourne and Rutland. I have greatly enjoyed myself at various light-hearted competitions on our smaller still waters, and in Bristol we have also run our annual bank competition on Chew. The relatively new Ruddles competition introduced a blend of boat and bank, and was also good fun.

I suppose the over-riding reason why I prefer boat fishing is that it has greater freedom. Some of the best traditions of past generations of anglers are preserved in loch style, and for this we should all be grateful. If the general interest in competitive fly fishing continues to grow, however, we shall find increasing pressures on boat bookings, even on the larger still waters. This factor alone could provoke further interest in bank competition, and this could in turn create a whole new substratum in the sport.

3 Sponsored Competitions

Youth Internationals

On 29 August 1985 a very important event took place at Llandegfedd reservoir in South Wales. This was the inaugural Youth International, fished between England and Wales, for anglers under 18 years of age. It represented an important step forward, not just for competitive fly fishing but also for the sport in general, as without a keen youth element there is little prospect for the future.

Many of us involved in the 'senior' Internationals had long felt that a youth competition was a good thing, and nobody was particularly surprised to see the level of enthusiastic response from youngsters in England and Wales. Equally heartening was the reaction of the many sponsors, whose generosity provided both help and prize money and enabled Moc Morgan to organise the first running of what is now an annual occasion.

It needs to be re-stated that this competition could not take place without sponsorship. Because of their totally amateur status national confederations simply do not have the funds to support the relatively high running costs of an event such as this, and whereas adult fly fishers can be expected to make a monetary contribution, it is not necessarily practical to ask youngsters to do so.

It says much for anglers, and those in ancillary or related trades, that the 1986 Youth International on Chew Valley Lake was even better supported. Interest from the angling youth was such that pre-qualifiers for the squads were needed, and donations were received from many clubs and individuals, as well as big companies. The event is now firmly on its feet. From this base, which currently looks like broadening to include Ireland, Scotland, and perhaps even France, young fly fishers can progress through to senior level with greater confidence. Their first taste of competition is rarely their last!

Benson & Hedges

A classic example of how big money sponsorship can be introduced into competitive fly fishing is to be found in the Benson & Hedges annual tournament. A member of Benson & Hedges' staff, Mike Perry, once stated that their aim was simply to elevate the status of fly fishing in the UK. They have achieved this, and much more besides.

Again, the principles are simple: this is a team competition, open to all registered club and associations in the four Home Countries. A series of regional elimination heats are held through the early months of the season, followed by National finals in July or August. The International final generally takes place in September. Full international loch style rules are in force, together with a few imaginative and sensible alterations.

The organisation of the tournament, together with the hospitality offered by Benson & Hedges, is impeccable. Indeed, it is the volume of organisational work, and *not* the prizes, that accounts for the vast majority of the competition budget. Apart from token prizes of fishing sweaters or similar items to the top individuals, the actual prize money goes to the club, and not to the team. The use of these monies is then at the discretion of the club, and in the past they have contributed towards disabled angler fishing, youth projects and the like. Individual financial gain is definitely not a leading aspect of the B & H!

There is no doubt in my mind that B & H have made a major contribution to the history of fly fishing. Primarily they have stimulated a great upsurge of interest in competitive fly fishing, with a corresponding increase in general angling awareness. More specifically, at a time when vast numbers of fly fishermen were resorting to large lead-headed lures to catch their fish, here was a competition that showed to the world just how effective the traditional methods really were.

In previous seasons fly tying classes in Bristol Reservoirs FFA were full of people tying lures. But suddenly all they wanted to learn about were 'legal size' buzzers, and nymphs, and wet fly patterns, just so that they could fish in the B & H.

Equally important is the way in which the tournament was, and is, presented to the public, both angling and general. The use of a public relations company to run the competition is a master-stroke, and one that ensures that all aspects of the fishing are presented in a palatable and entertaining fashion.

For the competitors themselves the B & H represents a highlight in the angling calendar. No other competition creates the same atmosphere, or engenders the same excitement. Anyone who has sampled the lavish hospitality provided will never forget it. For those who have not, let me paint a brief picture of the 1984 final, held in September on Rutland Water.

The 1984 Championship had captured the imagination of anglers everywhere. The level of excitement at every stage of the competition from the regional heats through to the semi-final was matched only by the depth of hospitality provided by Benson & Hedges. But even this left none of us prepared for the degree of our welcome at the final at Rutland Water.

Our day's practice fishing on Sunday yielded up a few of Rutland's secrets. My own team, BRFFA, had all fished Rutland before, but on such a vast expanse of water there will always be special conditions. Consequently the practice day was important in establishing a rough idea of tactics, a shortlist of flies, and a general assessment of the productive areas of the lake.

So often in competitions match day proves to be totally different from practice but, fortunately, conditions were near-identical on Monday, the first day of the competition. For the first time in any major tournament the fishing was staggered over two days, the first starting at 1 p.m. and finishing at 7.30 p.m. John Ketley released us at the appointed hour and it became obvious that a fair divergence of opinion existed as to where to go. There was a good split between the North and

John Ketley issues final instructions at a Benson & Hedges final.

South Arms, and a fair sprinkling heading towards the dam. My own team, having assessed the water the previous day, all opted for the North Arm and more or less as soon as we arrived we were into fish.

However, an early ripple gave way to almost flat calm conditions and the trout were obviously becoming reluctant during the afternoon. This was hardly surprising as with almost twenty boats ploughing among them they were becoming shy in the extreme. Fine tactics were called for and the successful anglers were those who scaled down to very light leaders and small buzzer patterns. Soldier Palmer took its fair share of fish, as did our own favourite fly, the Diawl Bach.

As evening approached an element of gamble came into the fishing. Should we stay where we were over a known holding

spot and risk losing the half-hour for the journey back? Or should we travel back to the lodge now and use what might be the best of the fishing between 6.30 and 7.30 p.m.? Most of us, displaying the angler's usual philosophy of sticking with moving fish, stayed put, and a good few fish came during that last hour.

We were all greeted at the water by a smart waiter offering glasses of whisky, but this was only a sampler of the entertainment to come. To say that Benson & Hedges looked after us lavishly is to understate the point. A spit-roast barbecue followed, along with every conceivable extra.

The half-way results were then announced and it quickly became clear that the first two places were fairly close. The local favourites, East Midlands Fly Fishers Association, had a 6lb advantage over my own team, who in turn had a 20lb advantage over the third place. We had 38 fish between us whilst East Midlands had 41, and so it was obvious that a sterling effort was needed by all concerned if we were to redress the balance on the second day. The second day, starting with bacon sandwiches at 6.30 a.m., yielded more than its fair share of walking wounded. For all that, the competitive element was very much to the fore and even the early hour could not dispel the nerves that usually come with a major competition. And again, we were breaking new ground in that boats had never been out at 7.30 a.m. on Rutland before.

Unfortunately the conditions were a far cry from the previous day, the nice gentle ripple being replaced by a strong and very chilly wind from the north-west. This put paid to any real hopes of a morning rise, and although even more boats headed for

Scrutineering at a big weigh-in.

the North Arm than the previous day it soon became apparent that the fish were not moving anything like as freely as they had been.

The competition on the second day was relatively short – only 5½ hours – and by mid-morning far fewer fish were being caught than had been anticipated. This meant that the result was likely to be even closer, and there were many anxious faces looking over shoulders to see if and where fish were being taken.

All too soon came the weigh-in, and this time we were greeted with hot punch at the landing stage, more than welcome in the chilly conditions. The actual result was still in doubt, and whilst we enjoyed the superb luncheon provided in the tented area following the weigh-in, there was an electric silence when Bob Williams finally got to his feet to announce our fate. In the event East Midlands had beaten us by a relatively comfortable 6lb as although they only had one fish more than us – 60 as against 61 – there was a good margin in terms of weight.

It had been in every way a prestige competition and all participants were keenly aware that Benson & Hedges are pioneering a totally new concept in competitive angling. Their organisation was immaculate, hospitality unique, and the warmth of the friendships generated made for a lasting experience. For our own part, we were proud to have been part of it all.

Since 1984 the competition has become a

truly international affair, with each of the Home Countries enjoying their own national final as a qualifier to the international competition. This gives an additional edge of excitement to the proceedings, and make for a very special event indeed.

It would be difficult to put a finger on quite why this competition is so popular, as it is probably due to a combination of many factors. To be successful six anglers have to work consciously and totally as a *team*, and must have complete confidence in each other. This is obviously true in the IFFA Internationals, but is somehow more intimate when done at club level, where team members are generally friends of long standing. That, and the total B & H atmos-

phere, is what sets this tournament apart from the rest.

World Fly Fishing Championship

Until the spring of 1987 relatively few people were even aware of the World Fly Fishing Championship, and fewer still knew much about it. Even those that did probably regarded it as having a European base – perhaps even bias – and the whole thing was just a bit too remote to generate any real interest. All that changed in 1987.

England had first taken part in the Championship in Spain in 1982, although it is fair to say that the five years leading

World Cup action – Moc Morgan nets a fish from the Test.

up to 1987 had seen them with little tangible success. The true high spot in the five years has to be Tony Pawson's magnificent individual performance when he won the individual World Champion title, again in Spain, in 1984.

The WFFC started modestly in 1981 and since then has progressed steadily each year, with ever more teams participating. The 1986 Championship in Belgium saw thirteen countries represented, yet sadly none of those teams were from outside Europe. However, all this was destined to change when it was announced that England was to be 'Host Nation' for 1987.

There are many evocative place names linked with fly fishing all over the world: Lake Taupo in New Zealand, the River Tormes in Spain and no end of famous spring creeks in America. But surely the most famous of them all has to be the crystal clear chalk stream, the River Test in England. Link this to the supreme quality of English stillwater fishing on Rutland and Grafham, spice the proceedings with the fascinating intimacy of Avington, complete the picture with a first-class organiser like Tony Pawson, and you have a recipe for something rather special. It seemed as though the World Fly Fishing Championship was destined to come of age.

The events that took place in late May of 1987 are now legendary. They will surely form the base and model for all future competition, although from a competi-

Are we taking things less than seriously? A Frenchman about to be baptised in the River Test.

tor's viewpoint it would be hard to see how the memories could possibly be bettered.

Preparations started early – way back in 1986 in fact – and from the outset it has to be said that without the phenomenal organising ability of that great man Tony Pawson things would never have happened as they did. Tony is a veteran of several WFFC encounters, as well as being a former England International under the IFFA banner. Although not large in stature, Tony has probably the biggest heart in fly fishing and is a veritable dynamo when it comes to work such as this. With the full backing and support of the Championship Committee, backed by the Salmon & Trout Association and the Confederation of English Fly Fishers, Tony set about the task of raising the vast amount of sponsorship needed to make England's hosting a unique occasion. In the event 21 nations were destined to compete and the sheer physical logistics of accommodation, transport, and administration were daunting.

Initially the choice of venues posed little problem. It was agreed that the main Team Championship would be decided over two days' loch style fishing on both Grafham and Rutland. The number of competitors plus the fact that no single venue could accommodate upwards of 100 anglers made a two-day split essential. Northampton would be the host town and once the Team Championship was decided, the whole entourage would move to Winchester for the top 32 rods to decide the Individual Champion, again fishing alternate days on the River Test at Kimbridge and at Avington.

Still back in 1986, the problem of selecting England's team arose. Due to the vast popularity of loch style competitive fly fishing in England there was a vast pool of eligible anglers who could be called upon, and the process of selection was not easy. In the event, selection was a joint effort between the WFFC Committee, the Confederation of English Fly Fishers, and the Salmon & Trout Association, all of whom would have to choose a non-fishing captain, the five team members and the two reserves. To ensure the strongest possible team, those selected had to have proved their competence by fishing at least twice for England in CEFF Internationals, and also had to have experience in river and small stillwater fishing. They finally settled upon Geoff Clarkson as captain, and a team of Bob Church, Brian Leadbetter, John Pawson, Dennis Buck and (I am proud to say) myself. The two reserves of Brian Thomas and Bob Morey were, to all intents and purposes, part of the team as they would attend every function, including the team practice sessions.

I can honestly say that never before or since have I experienced such team spirit in a group of anglers. Right from the start we worked almost as one, and preparations began as far back as September 1986 when the initial meetings took place. It was agreed, at a very informal fishing day on Rutland, that if England were to have a chance against such outstanding world competition then a total and thorough series of practice days would be needed. We needed not only to be familiar with the waters themselves, and with the likely conditions that we would encounter in May, but also to be really in tune with each other.

It is all too easy for an outsider to say that there was a home advantage in 1987, as indeed there had been in every year of the WFFC. However, loch style is an internationally-recognised fishing method,

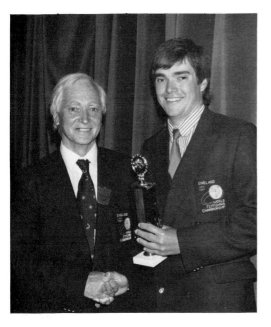

*Father and son Tony and John Pawson –
organiser and competitor.*

and with the calibre of some of the overseas visitors nothing could be left to chance, and there was certainly no room for any kind of complacency. With great skill Geoff Clarkson therefore put together a training programme that was designed to cover every eventuality. For the four weekends leading up to the Championship the team alternated between Grafham and Rutland, and even managed a 'sampler day' on the River Itchen. We were as well-prepared to meet the challenge as any team could possibly have been. This is how it was:

As ever the social side of things played a very big part in the initial stages, and as the teams gathered at the Northampton Moat House Hotel for the opening ceremonies there were familiar smiles on equally familiar faces. Where anglers are involved there is no such thing as a language barrier, and one could see animated sign language 'conversations' taking place on all sides.

The serious side revealed itself on the Friday morning, when final practice started in earnest. This was the first chance to put the transport arrangements to the test, and things went incredibly smoothly. Each team had a volunteer courier and their own minibus transport. Throughout the Championship to the eternal credit of those involved no single competitor was either lost or late in turning up at the prescribed venue.

The first match day was Saturday 23 May, and the fickle English weather left everyone wondering if spring was really just a figment of the weathermen's imagination. On Rutland and Grafham, chill winds coupled with misty drizzle and very low temperatures meant that few fish were likely to be found on the surface. Sinking lines of various densities were the order of the day, as almost all the fish had their heads well down.

On Grafham, where I was drawn with an engaging Irishman named John O'Malley, we also had coloured water to contend with, and I found myself stuck with sunk line tactics that are fairly alien to my normal angling philosophy. Fish were hard to come by, and it was pretty much a case of concentration and work rate. Even so, the occasional fish did show itself, and despite the sinking line an accurate 'snap cast' would produce results.

Over at Rutland it was quickly evident that nobody else had found the pocket of fish that the English had discovered on practice day, and Brian Leadbetter and

The author in action at the World Fly Fishing Championship,
tense moments as an eight pounder comes to the net.

John Pawson had the North Arm more or less to themselves. They left the competition far behind, with both of them weighing-in over thirty fish apiece for the top two places.

Bob Church and I also had the top two spots between us at Grafham, with Dennis Buck a close fifth, which meant that the England squad had an almost unassailable lead at the end of the first day.

On the second day we had much brighter conditions to cope with at Rutland, and with gin-clear water it was obviously going to be tough going. Added to this, the bush telegraph had been working overtime, and just about every boat in the competition headed up the North Arm. The fish were close in to the banks, requiring careful positioning of the boats and a lot of engine work that quickly put the trout down. After that it was again a question of a lot of hard work for relatively little reward.

Grafham's second day saw Brian Leadbetter again as top rod, and with a steady performance from the rest of the team the Championship title was ours. The mood was understandably euphoric, and the evening banquet at the Moat House was quite an occasion. Despite our win, by far the biggest cheer of the night went to the ever-popular Australians in second place. Their team had endeared itself to everyone, and their instant mastery of a style that was totally new to them was extremely impressive. The New Zealanders came third, with a classic comment from their captain, Terry Entwistle, that if they had to lose it was good to do so to 'one of our offshore islands'.

In spite of a serious crop of hangovers, the following day saw the whole show travelling south to Hampshire for lunch at the Mayfly pub on the River Test. The transformation could not have been more complete; we left the dark chill behind us and moved into high temperatures and bright sunshine – spring at last! Most competitors could now relax and enjoy the infinite variety of fishing that had been arranged on waters throughout the county. But for the top 32 rods, the final process of selecting the individual World Champion was just beginning.

This was where the true spirit of the England team really showed. Almost incredibly, all five of us had qualified for the section, and we had agreed that, just as in the team event, we would pool and share all our information. Thus the Avington specialists tied flies for the river men, and vice versa, which meant that we were all well briefed. Added to this, we all drew benefit from our team mentor, Charles Jardine, who had been on hand with verbal and practical fly-tying advice throughout the Championship.

My first day draw was for Avington, and weather conditions were perfect. Only occasional ripples disturbed the water's surface, and in the calm periods it was obvious that a fairly generous stocking had taken place. Each angler had to fish eight half-hour sessions, moving around two pegs at each change-over, thus ensuring a fair spread of fishing on all three lakes. My first peg had to be regarded as 'pole position', and yielded seven fish including a brace that weighed 15lb between them. All very well, but the points system only allowed for 4½lb as a maximum size, so I had to weigh the thrill of these big fish against the time taken to subdue them.

The author's best-ever brace in competition at Avington WFFC, 1987. The stupid grin tells all.

Luckily, Bob Church and I were drawn alongside each other all day, which meant that we could keep in touch and exchange views. As well as being an exceptionally fine angler, Bob is a great enthusiast for competition, and we were able to motivate each other throughout – all of which added to the spice! At the final whistle we had again scored first and second places on the lake.

On the Test Brian Leadbetter had proved his all-round versatility yet again by notching up another 'top gun', with Dennis second, and John Pawson third.

The outcome was virtually decided at this point in time, with Brian holding an almost invincible lead. Only a near-disaster at Avington on the next day could

The author receives a WFFC trophy from Luciana Lynch.

rob him of the title, although all of us were determined to give him a run for his money. Friendship prevailed, and we were still tying flies for each other on the morning of the final day.

The Test was every bit as exciting as predicted, and the morning saw most anglers taking fish. The Humbert family at Kimbridge Farm had donated their water, and we had heard a rumour during the previous day of a 'buffet to end all buffets' at lunchtime. But I can honestly say that never in my business life, which has taken me to many gastronomic events in Europe,

have I see a buffet like this one. Lobster, gravadlax, crevettes, salmon, fresh Kimbridge asparagus – the list is endless, and the tables were covered from end to end.

After such a feast the afternoon session saw several of us fishing rather more sedately, though with undiminished diligence. The French showed their competence on rivers, thoroughly enjoying themselves and catching several of the beautifully-marked brownies, whilst Bob and I managed to pull in some of the better rainbows.

Brian Leadbetter could not quite make it

The victorious England team in the WFFC of 1987 outside Winchester Cathedral.

a 'perfect' performance, finishing third at Avington behind what was a great day for John Pawson. Nevertheless, this was more than enough to clinch the individual title for him, richly deserved after such a remarkable display of consistency. Perhaps better still was the fact that the English team had taken five of the first six places, a fairytale result that could never have been predicted, and may well never be repeated.

The final evening, at Winchester Civic Hall, passed all too quickly. Some wonderful memories linger, with so many new friendships made, and thoughts and theories exchanged. Celebrations ran on well into the night, the Australian bush hats being passed from head to head almost as swiftly as the brimming trophies, with everyone sharing in the champagne.

The following morning saw many of our number in the hotel lounges with mixed emotions. It was over, but nobody wanted it to end. Anyone who was part of it all will surely never forget the experience, with pictures in the mind's eye retaining their clarity long after the official photographs have faded.

Such is the atmosphere generated at a top level competition, although it is virtually impossible to describe in words. However, it fully supports those early principles that angler should talk to angler in a spirit of friendship and understanding. All barriers of race, creed, colour and language are torn down, leaving only a common denominator of those seeking fulfilment from their angling, and sharing both failure and success. If the World Fly Fishing Championship can further such principles on a truly international scale then our sport will be that much richer, and future generations will be able to share in the kind of fellowship that only a fly fishing competition can bring.

The World Cup – Lough Mask

It could well be said that no fisherman should consider himself a *complete* competition angler until he has fished in Ireland. Furthermore, it is beyond question that the greatest competition held in the Emerald Isle is the Lough Mask World Cup, and all anglers who have experienced the unique atmosphere of this great event come away with vivid and lasting memories.

Having not yet taken part in the World Cup – something I intend to put right very shortly – I asked someone who really knows it well to describe it for this book. Peter Thomas is the natural, inevitable choice: he has fished Mask many times, and has distinguished himself greatly in the results sheets. As well as his experiences in Ireland, Peter is an international angler of great standing. He has captained England in an IFFA match, and lives within a stone's throw of Rutland, where he is an acknowledged expert. He is perhaps

best known for his top-of-the-water style, which is a treat to watch, and obviously stands him in good stead in Ireland. This, then, is his account of one World Cup.

The twenty-third World Open Wet-Fly Championship (the World Cup), organised so capably by the Committee of the relatively small Ballinrobe and District Angling Club, was once again held on Lough Mask, County Mayo in 1987. Traditionally, the competition is run over the Irish bank holiday period on the first weekend of August. At stake is the World Cup, plus a formidable list of perpetual cups, trophies and replicas, and a vast multitude of other prizes.

What makes this event so special is the opportunity to fish for truly wild brown trout on a large unpolluted natural water in the company, both on and off the water, of such kind and friendly folk. Despite the stakes and the prestige that goes with the event, both for the competitors and indeed the boatmen, the atmosphere is one of relaxed excitement and anticipation.

The competition runs over five days: four days of heats from Thursday to Sunday, followed by the final on the Monday. The Committee endeavours to allow competitors to fish their heat on their chosen day. There was a record 428 entries for the 1987 competition. The heats ultimately produced, on a daily pro-rata basis, 109 anglers for the final. Organising this number of competitors is a feat in itself, more so when most of the boats assembled for the competition are 'imported' and privately owned. Chances are the owners will be competing, as well as making their boats and themselves available during the competition.

An open draw is made in advance for

partners and boatmen, and if it is at all possible visitors are drawn to fish with local anglers. There is, of course, considerable interest and drama generated by the draw, and what better place to publish them than in the local pubs? As if one were needed, the draw provides a ready-made excuse to visit the bar, to satisfy your curiosity and at the same time build up your strength with a drop of the black stuff.

The rules of the competition are straightforward. Basically they are: not less than two and not more than four flies (no hook size limitation). Only one rod assembled, 12-foot size limit. Fishing is essentially loch style from a free-drifting boat – the drift being controlled by the boatman. Any other type of drift control device would not be practicable because you are searching for fish that are lurking around the rocks in comparatively shallow water. It is uncanny how the boatman with consummate skill and experience is able, by gentle and subtle movement of the oar behind the boat, to steer the boat safely through and around submerged and visible rocks with delicacy and precision even in a very strong wind and heavy wave. A great deal of your success will be due to your boatman's efforts.

Each day's fishing is from 11 a.m. until 6 p.m., starting and finishing from Cushlough. It is easy to be deceived at the start by the relatively calm conditions existing in the bay at Cushlough. The bay lies on the eastern shore and has a comparatively narrow outlet to the north-west, so there is a natural barrier protecting it from the prevailing south-westerly winds. Of all the sights I have seen in competitions there can be none more dramatic and spectacular than the armada of fifty or more speeding boats leaving the shelter of the bay and meeting the full force and strength of Mask. With great regard and respect for the Lough, boatmen sensibly reduce power. I have seen anglers 'crossing' themselves at this moment – it is open to question as to whether they do this in hope of success or self-preservation. The boats then disperse and set course towards their crews' mutually agreed fishing areas; places with evocative names like the Black Rocks, Lively Bay, Devenish, Caher Bay and, to the south where the Masks leaks out, the ominously named Cong Canal.

The fishing technique most commonly seen is quite a short line and an almost immediate 'lift' – the bob fly then being held as long as possible on or near the surface. In a strong wind some anglers resort to heavier and therefore much thinner fast sinking lines, in order to achieve better control of their flies. My personal preference is a well-used WF6 floating line, the tip of which tends to sink slightly. You will see local anglers with fairly large and well-hackled flies in use, including Green Peters, Murrough variants, Mayflies and Mayfly nymphs, Daddy-long-legs and Bumbles. The Bumble is a new one for me. One variation, the Claret Bumble, is a very heavily dressed fly with a claret seal's fur body, fully palmered claret hackle, and a short blue wing. Another version has an olive green dressing with a blue jay hackle.

After each day's fishing the weigh-in is conducted quickly and efficiently. In typical Irish fashion competitors string and tag their fish which are then hung on a rack for all to see – a sight which arouses considerable speculation among both spectators and competitors alike as to the results.

Another nice idea – and it's included in

Tackle preparation – knots are triple-checked for competition.

the entrance fee – is that the competitors from each day's heat join up and have supper together at one of the hotels in Ballinrobe. And very animated these affairs can be after the events and traumas of the day. Those lucky and fortunate enough to have qualified will, by their success, get another 'free' day's fishing in the Final and an invitation to the Dinner Dance and Presentation.

With the end of the competition the Committee have a mammoth task in sorting out and putting names to all the prizes. The 1987 winner received, in addition to the World Cup and replica, an 18ft 10in fibreglass lake boat, complete with a 9.9hp Johnson outboard engine, and a very impressive cut glass trophy. There were then 23 further trophies and prizes. The second prize was a cup and a replica, a 6hp outboard engine, and two cheques for £100. The 23rd prize was a cheque for £20. I hasten to add that these prizes were based on the aggregate weight of fish caught on the final day. There were, in addition, some thirty or more other prizes including heat winners, best fish, and overseas categories. Also, the winners of the first three major prizes on the final day are not necessarily eligible to receive additional prizes from the results of the qualifying days. This provides for a more even spread and number of winners.

With great style and sense of showmanship the Committee contrive to get the winner's boat into the dining hall. This is then bedecked with all the other trophies and prizes, capped of course by the impressive silver World Cup. As the inevitably long presentation continues the boat is gradually emptied of its contents, the World Cup and boat presentation being saved to the end.

On a personal note, and certainly with regard to the UK trout scene, I am amongst those who have fears and worries over the award of individual prize money in trout fishing competitions, and the possible 'corruption' of an angler's philosophy and attitude to his sport. I am most gratified to report that I have not seen the slightest evidence of this occurring in the Irish trout fishing scene, and they have been doing it for a long time!

The results of the 1987 event typically show the difficulty and challenge the competitor has to face. Only 65 fish weighing 85.64lb were caught by the 109 competitors on the final day. Nevertheless, the event will remain a very special part of my fishing calendar, not only for the opportunity to catch truly wild browns, but for the pleasure and atmosphere created by the organisers, the competitors and the people of Ballinrobe.

4 Loch Style Tackle

There is a lot of unnecessary and irrelevant mystique surrounding tackle for competitive loch style fishing. Some of it has grown around one or two celebrated exponents of the art, in that their very personal style has meant that many others have followed their lead, copying their tackle rig to the finest detail. However, it must be remembered that one man's meat is another's poison, and whilst a 12-foot converted carp pole might suit Bob Draper very well it certainly will not do for those of lesser build or varying ability.

Fishermen are nothing if not individuals, and thus we all have our own preferences when it comes to choosing rod and line. Indeed, of all the aspects of our sport the tackle we use is the most personal, reflecting our style as well as our idiosyncracies, and our choice is influenced by whim, advertising and bank balance – probably in that order!

It is a well-known fact that the average fly fisherman will see his wife and children on the breadline before he forsakes the purchase of the latest fly rod on the mar-

The author nets a good fish at Rutland, North Arm.

ket. As a breed we are easy prey for the marketing men, especially for the 'Mark II mentality'. They make tiny, cosmetic changes, call it the Mark II, and suddenly we just *have* to have it. After all, a change in the reel seat is *bound* to improve our casting, isn't it?

Of course, such comments are frivolous and are intended to be so. However, there is very little frivolity displayed when an angler is at the tackle shop counter. Few items can be regarded as cheap these days, and the purchase of any piece of equipment represents a serious decision. In the case of major items like rod and reel you are making an investment in your sport for many years to come, and with top manufacturers offering a lifetime guarantee on their products it is indeed an important choice.

So just how good is the current market for loch style tackle, and are all the developments as fundamental as some manufacturers would have us believe? Also, is there such a thing as an 'ideal' competitive outfit, suitable for all eventualities? Not all the innovations are as new as the makers claim, and neither will they perform as well as some of the extravagant sales brochures say they do. It would also be a great mistake for any angler to follow the prescribed rig of any great 'expert', as the resulting outfit might be totally unsuitable for another person. Although all component items are interrelated, it is better at this stage to take them individually.

The Line

Most people seem to start with a rod, and work their way through the rest of the gear from there. Instead, I would like to start with what I regard as the single most important factor in loch-style tackle – line weight.

For many seasons I have been advocating a return to the first principles of fly fishing. Quite simply, the backbone of this philosophy involves deriving as much pleasure as possible from the act of catching fish, and this applies equally to both competitive outings and a normal day afloat. To my mind, these pleasures are increased many times over by the use of lighter and finer tackle. For loch style today, and bearing in mind the range of quality rods on the market, there is absolutely no need to use a line weight heavier than AFTM 6. There need be no great preoccupation with distance when fishing from a boat, at least in the majority of situations. Presentation is everything, and the accent is firmly placed on accuracy, coupled with a lack of surface disturbance.

Carry the logic of this one stage further, and it follows that an AFTM weight of 5 or 6 will make less disturbance when it lands on the water than would a rating of 8 or 9. The line is lighter and slimmer, and as a bonus it is also easier to control. The fact that to cast such a line will, by definition, require a lighter and more sensitive rod is a happy coincidence. Even in a strong wind there is no real problem in using a lighter line, although in rough conditions the advantages of presentation are somewhat negated by a heavy wave. Competitions often involve a number of boats fishing in one area, with fish becoming spooky and sensitive to any form of disturbance. It therefore follows that the line which lands with the minimum of fuss is far less likely to scare the fish, and better results may follow.

A good fish from Rutland's South Arm.

In the field of fly lines it is largely a case of 'you get what you pay for'. The better-quality lines are, as a general rule, the most expensive. I happen to have a preference for either Cortland or Orvis for the floaters, Scientific Anglers for the intermediate (the sink rate is just right for loch style), and Masterline or Scientific Anglers for the less important sinkers. I say less important because there is little that cannot be achieved with a floating line, and a sinker has some fundamental restrictions when fished from a drifting boat. The depth at which your flies are presented to the fish can be controlled by leader length, fly weight, and leader construction. I accept that in early or late season, or in times of very cold water, a fast-sinking line may be required, but these occasions are few. I use a floating line for upwards of eighty per cent of my competitive fishing, and it takes fairly extreme circumstances to tempt me into using a sinker.

A logical extension at the business end of the fly line is a braided leader, and in my opinion these are among the most significant developments of recent years, giving genuine improvement to both casting and presentation. The basic principle is that a braided section leader offers smoother turn-over between fly line and tippet. It does this by ensuring a progressive transmission of energy from the unfurling fly line, thereby controlling the loop of the leader. In practice it works even better than it sounds, and with a floating line it gives vastly improved presentation, which in turn offers greater accuracy.

Braided leaders are either straight-through tapers or in braided sections joined by tiny loops. The advantage of the latter is that a weighted section can be added, effectively making a sink tip fly line redundant, and offering greater flexibility in terms of the depth at which your fly is fishing. I commend them to you wholeheartedly.

The Reel

I have never subscribed to the school of thought that a reel is simply a storage reservoir for the fly line. The use of a good-quality reel is a pleasure in itself, and having confidence that it will not stick or jam at the critical moment must surely justify any extra expenditure.

That said, I should add that there is a huge variation in the price of reels. At the inexpensive end of the market it is hard to beat the new Speedex or Condex models from Shakespeare. These are serviceable and reliable fly reels, offering every facility that the angler could require, and they represent incredible value for money. At the other end of the scale it is perfectly possible to part with a substantial three-figure sum for a precision-engineered, hand-built model from someone like Ari Hart in Holland. Anyone who has seen these 'designer reels' will know that they are things of great beauty; they are quite genuinely a lifetime investment, as they will probably outlive the angler, and in time may well become a family heirloom.

The middle ground is, as ever, inhabited by the greater numbers. In Britain the long pedigree of tradition that Hardy have established in fly reel design is still there, and will appeal to many people. As always, you pay your money and take your choice, but be sure above all that the reel balances the rest of your outfit. A reel that is too light for your rod is just as much of a problem as one that is too heavy, as this impedes casting, and ultimately leads to fatigue.

The Rod

So to the biggest, most important, and potentially most expensive item of equipment – the fly rod. The newcomer to competitions, or to loch style fishing in general, might well find the range and variety of rods available at best bewildering, and at worst downright confusing. Without some degree of advice he may easily find himself with the wrong tool for the job, and be left disillusioned and disappointed.

The development of the carbon-fibre or graphite rod over the last 20 years, a period that has seen more innovation in fly rod design than the last 200, has undoubtedly changed the whole face of fly fishing. There are still devotees of cane rods, although they are few and must pay a high premium for their privilege; most cane rods are now made to special order, and cost perhaps three times their nearest graphite counterpart. Glass fibre also has its place, but again there are few who would prefer glass against the obvious benefits of the lightness, versatility and power of graphite.

I genuinely believe that the development of graphite has probably gone as far as it reasonably can, and the Kevlar and

Bob Church slips over, but the fish is in the net.

Total concentration at Avington.

other graphite mixes could well be said to be simply change for change's sake. The products on offer to fishermen are as near perfect as makes no matter and leave very little room for further improvement. The technology now available to individual manufacturers, coupled with the varying grade and quality of graphite used, is largely responsible for the staggering price range that exists for a rod. Currently, there are graphite rods available for £30 to £300, with some very good products in the lower range of that span.

The stillwater boom of the past generation has meant that vast numbers of new fishermen have taken up the sport, as bank fishing is readily and, in relative terms, cheaply available on most major water supply reservoirs. However, in compara-

tive terms boat fishing is expensive, and only a fairly small proportion of stillwater anglers are involved in loch style fishing. Yet although the number is small it is growing very rapidly, and as a consequence manufacturers of rod ranges which were previously weighted towards the bank angler are now showing increased listings for rods suitable for loch style.

Whilst I am a staunch advocate of 'the light approach' it still needs to be said that a rod length of 9½ feet should be regarded as the minimum for successful loch style – 10½ is arguably the optimum length. Anything longer and the rod becomes cumbersome to a degree, and anything shorter does not really permit the flexibility of approach, particularly for surface dibbling. As with any rule there are always notable exceptions, and I am fully aware that several highly successful competition anglers use 12-foot rods (the maximum length permitted under international rules) with consummate ease. However even they would admit that they are in the minority, and I dread to think of the state of their wrists after a full day's fishing.

So, if we follow the light line philosophy to its logical conclusion we are looking for a 10 or 10½-foot rod capable of handling an AFTM 5 or 6 weight line. The rod must have inherent subtlety, yet also posess the reserve power to cope with high winds and bigger than average fish, these two factors sometimes occurring simultaneously. Essentially the rod must be light, to enable the angler to fish a complete day without fatigue. Still more important, it must become an extension of the angler's own arm, transmitting even the remotest touch from a fish at maximum range.

To be honest there are only very few rods that meet this specification. No criticism of rod makers is implied here, for they quite naturally have been supplying the needs of those whose demand was for ever longer distance casting from the bank. The bulk of the market is there, and they have understandably been happy to oblige.

However, preoccupation with distance casting alone is not to be recommended, particularly in competition. To the Scots and Irish, who pursue the short-lining style, twenty yards is a long cast, as they prefer to work their flies through a relatively short path towards the boat, enticing the trout into action by the 'life' that they and their rods can impart to the flies. Nevertheless, for all-round versatility the competition fisher must always have the reserve of a long cast, and therefore his rod must be a genuine all-rounder.

Because of this fairly exacting specification it is no real surprise to find that the rods that truly fit the bill are on the expensive side. In my opinion those rods of Orvis, Sage, Bruce and Walker, and to a lesser extend Hardy, are all worthy of consideration. To be subjective for a moment, there are many reasons why I personally favour Orvis. Orvis is an American manufacturer, and the general preference in America is for shorter, lighter rods, and they regard anything over 9½ feet as heavy. They tend, rather unjustly, to regard British stillwater fishing as being a touch brutal, especially as they have little to compare it with, as most of their fishing is on moving water. Even so, the Orvis rods have developed a wonderful through action that is truly delightful, and very reminiscent of cane. They have so much more life to them than most of their British-made counterparts, a factor that is not lost on the growing band of UK Orvis owners. Their 10½-foot loch style rod is supreme.

On calmer days and specifically in conditions of flat calm I suggest that a 9½-foot rod is more than adequate. Again, light conditions require light tactics, and you will quickly find that the fish share this sentiment. I accept that a rod of this length will cut across many people's idea of loch style, and the only way I can justify this is by quoting results. There is no doubt in my mind that this short rod has won several major competitions for me, and has helped to catch fish that might otherwise have been missed.

I have experienced many competition days when near-calm conditions prevailed, such as the Benson & Hedges final at Bewl Bridge in 1986. Many anglers using heavier tactics came in clean, but dry fly work with size 14 flies and a 5 weight line proved a winning combination. Without the lighter rod such tactics would have been virtually unworkable.

I also have a great aversion to stiff-action rods, which I find totally at odds with my fishing philosophy. The principal benefit of light line tactics stems from the ability of any rod to fish ultra fine tippets. The stiffer rods just do not have the ability to cushion the strike when fishing with points of 3lb and below. They are not sensitive enough, and neither is there enough resilience in their action to avoid a break. Conversely, the softer rod offers supreme sensitivity, even at long range, and with practice you will find that you can use very fine tippets indeed with every confidence. All the other benefits, such as the true feel of playing a fish, the ability to place the fly with pin-point accuracy, and the sheer pleasure of casting stem from this one basic principle.

One final point here concerns the ringing of a rod, and this is of particular importance to those who prefer to 'build their own'. Building your own rod, essentially a low-cost option which enables you to personalise the rod to your own requirements, has many advantages. You can have a first-class rod for a fraction of the manufacturer's price, choosing your own level of adornment in terms of reel seat and fittings. But the rings are *vitally important*. Do not be misled by the extravagant claims of the makers of ceramic rings, or guides as they are sometimes called. Many tests have proved that top quality, stainless steel snake rings give appreciably less friction than their ceramic counterparts. Basically this is because they have a smaller surface area in contact with the fly line. It is for this reason that almost all the

top quality rods from America feature snake guides – it is a matter of preference, rather than cost.

The Leader

It is a great paradox of fly fishing that one of the most important items of equipment should also be one of the cheapest. The leader, or tippet, should be the last thing that a trout sees before he is hooked. Indeed, if you have done the job properly he won't see it at all, as the main aim is to present the fly in such a way as to give it a totally convincing and lifelike appearance.

Different angling situations require different leader set-ups, and the variations are almost infinite. But before we look at leader rigs, it is worth pausing for a moment to consider the material itself. Nylon monofilament has come a long way since the days of the old gut casts, and here again there are recent developments that have contributed greatly to our sport. There are now commercially-tied leaders available, either in pre-knotted format, or with a natural taper whereby the nylon gradually decreases in diameter. The purpose in this and all cases is to give smooth turnover, and consequently better presentation.

The reason that most serious competition anglers prefer to tie their own leaders is simply because we get through too many of them! Competition rules allow a maximum of three droppers, and naturally tapering leaders are not geared to cope with this. On breezy days wind knots can and do occur, and these need to be removed from the rig for safety's sake. Indeed, many competitors forsake any kind

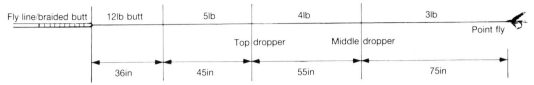

Leader rigged for standard team of wet flies. This is a typical rig for most competition situations, and covers most eventualities. When using four flies, distances are 36in 12lb butt; 36in to top dropper; 45in to middle dropper; 60in to point.

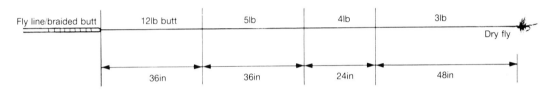

Leader rigged for standard dry fly (stillwater). The rig has a tapered leader for single dry fly fishing.

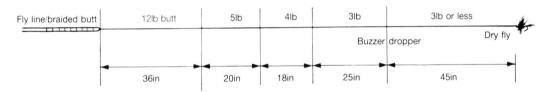

Leader rigged for buzzer/dry fly technique (stillwater). This is a 'hedged bet' rig for calm or near calm conditions. A very small buzzer of size 14–18 is used, on a 2in dropper. The leader is then greased, but the 2in dropper is not. Frequently the dry fly acts as a 'strike indicator', when the buzzer is taken by a fish.

of taper at all, and simply use straight-through nylon of the same strength, for the whole of the leader.

Personally, I prefer to taper by steps as I find that this gives better turnover, especially when used with a braided butt. Essentially, there are three types of leader rig for competition, all of which are illustrated below. The exact lengths in each will vary, depending on wind and general conditions, and the overall length is a matter for subjective choice. The ground rule is to use the maximum length of leader with which you are comfortable and confident, the basic premise being that the further your flies are from the fly line, the better. As a rough figure my overall wet fly leader length will vary from 18 feet minimum, through to around 25 feet. Consequently, it is not the prescribed lengths that matter in these diagrams but rather the proportion. In all cases the 12lb butt is joined to a braided butt section with Superglue, although there are many who join the 12lb butt to the flyline by using a nail knot.

My own standard competition rig employs two droppers, rather than three as favoured by so many Scots. I find a team of three flies more manageable than four, but this must remain a purely personal observation. However, you should remember that if you intend to use a double hook under international rules this counts as *two* flies – so beware!

Leaders are not nearly as complicated as some people would have you believe; they are largely a matter of common sense. I have a distinct preference for lighter tippet diameters, because fish find them difficult to see and also because this fits in well with my light-line philosophy. Not everyone gets on with fine tippets, and so the rule is just the same as for leader length – use the finest that you find comfortable, and in which you are confident.

The relatively new double-strength materials on the market are very useful, as they enable us to fish finer than would

otherwise be the case. In general, though, they have one inherent disadvantage in that they have a greater degree of shine in their finish – conventional material has a duller matt finish. To be effective this shine needs to be removed by using any of the proprietary fuller's earth mixes or leader treatments.

For obvious reasons of space I do not propose to look at every item of tackle available on the market. The competition angler should be well-equipped in terms of waterproof clothing, polarising sunglasses, waistcoat and the like. In the final analysis the subject of tackle comes down to two simple factors – personal preference and bank balance. No rod or outfit will directly improve an angler's casting ability, but what it will do is hugely increase his enjoyment of the sport. It is rather like the difference between house red and chateau-bottled claret – they are both bottles of wine, but there the resemblance ends. An angler using the best tackle that he can afford will find that his confidence is proportionately increased, and confidence, as we all know, is a vital element in competitive fly fishing.

5 Competition Basics

Practice Day

A lot of people, or more particularly a lot of wives, tend to think that a practice day is just another excuse for an extra day's fishing, and regard it as a rather unnecessary adjunct to any competition. To a certain extent this is true. Whilst practice days are a very necessary part of any competition, they should not be taken too seriously. It is best to aim for a very light-hearted practice day on the water, saving your full concentration for the match itself.

The idea of a practice day has long been a part of the IFFA Home International Series. Thursday and Friday are the two practice days, with the main event on the Saturday. The theory is that everyone has a chance to get to know the water concerned, sort out a few successful flies, and get to know the main fish-holding areas. It is important that the angler catches at least one or two fish on practice day to give him confidence for the match day itself.

My own approach to practice day is essentially very relaxed. However, I still regard it as an essential part of the proceedings and I usually give it a fair amount of thought. Depending on the water's size I like to fish in as many different parts of it as is reasonably possible, although on large lakes this is not always a viable proposition; this is where the team practice comes into play. Whilst on smaller venues such as Draycote it is quite feasible for every angler to fish the whole lake on practice day, the larger lakes are best divided into specific areas, with each team member taking his boat to one allotted region. Ideas can then be pooled at lunchtime and again in the evening, so that everyone has a clear picture of what is going on and where. This very basic ploy is one that has worked well for many seasons, and is practised by most serious clubs in the Benson & Hedges competition, and indeed in the Home International series. In the latter, as teams of fourteen anglers are involved, we are able to pin people down to relatively small areas in practice sessions, and we are thus able to check each location, and also assess the validity of sinking, floating and Intermediate lines in any one spot. In this way a comprehensive picture of fish-holding areas, feeding times and preferred fly patterns can be built up.

Over recent years, and as a by-product of many happy and successful competitions, a little ritual has evolved over the eve of match day itself. It is quite simply a last-minute fly-tying session. There is nothing quite like fishing a match day with flies specifically tied to fish on that particular venue, at that particular time of year, and in a way proven to be successful on practice day. The flies tied will be those that I, and perhaps my fellow team members, have found to be the killing pattern on practice day, and as such I will have supreme confidence in them on match day. To this end, I find that one of the most vital pieces of equipment is a portable fly-tying kit. Obviously this need not be anywhere near as elaborate as the domestic system. It should contain the barest of essentials in terms of tools, and a skeleton kit of the various items of fur and feather found to be most in use. In our BRFFA team, we have three fly-tyers of some note and they are kept well supplied with amber fluid by the other three non-tying members; an interesting and enjoyable evening is thus assured, and one that sees all of us totally prepared for the day to come.

Enjoyable as practice day should be, however, it seems to me rather unnecessary to burn the midnight oil at the bar. You will have, after all, been preparing for match day for some time, and to attempt to fish seriously with any sort of hangover is surely a pointless waste. I know of at least one Bristol angler who once attended a National final and was so much the worse for wear that he did not even leave his bed until noon on match day, thereby forfeiting both a day's fishing and any chance of representing his country in the following year. A couple of pints are fine, but leave the heavy drinking for the celebrations!

Match Day

For many, match day represents the culmination of many months waiting and preparation, and indeed in a major competition it may well be the highlight of a whole season.

There are so many aspects to the final preparations on match day that I have devised a very simple check-list for myself, so that nothing is left to chance. Without this mental (or written) check-list, it is quite possible to get into your boat having forgotten something vital like a landing net, a fly box or even, as happened to an Irish boat partner once, a rod! To make absolutely sure I check everything twice, and in a prescribed sequence: rod, reels, flies, clothing, net and tackle bag – it's that simple, and that sure! On match day anything that *can* go wrong *will* go wrong. The only antidote to this is total and complete preparation, extending from the obvious check-list above, right down to the construction of pre-tied leaders.

I don't know whether it's nerves, over-enthusiasm, or whatever, but I invariably seem to manage to make a complete mess of my leader within the first fifteen minutes of every major competition. Accordingly, it is a very necessary part of the preparation sequence to tie up at least two spare leaders, in the rigs most appropriate for the day in question. For instance, on a day of calm or near-calm conditions, you may well start with a standard three-fly cast, but drop down quickly to either a dry fly rig, or perhaps a single buzzer on a long leader. It will save time and frustration if you have both leaders tied and ready for instant use. Hang on to your old leader spools for this purpose, as they make excellent storage units. In the same vein, most of us get tangled at some stage during the day, especially in a stiff wind, and it is far easier to prepare a spare leader in the relative calm of the car park, rather than when the wind is taking the nylon pieces all over the place in the boat.

Match day is also the wrong time to spend an age gazing blankly into the fly box. I know of a great number of anglers who possess upwards of a thousand flies at any one time, stored in maybe six or seven different boxes. This is fine for a day's leisure fishing, but the syndrome of being 'spoiled for choice' has no place in a big competition. Rather, you should have a workable shortlist, the net result of your findings on practice day, all in one place and ready to hand. To this end, I prefer to use my 'black box', a small and convenient fly box that holds no more than fifty favourites of the moment. In this way, fly selection is immediate and positive. Of course, this in no way prevents you from taking all reserve fly boxes along with you – things can quite easily change overnight, and you should never be without some second-line ideas!

Most aspects of tactics are covered in the following chapter. However, some fundamental principles need to be stated here, as they fall under the general heading of common sense, rather than specific tactics.

Netting

To begin with, I would firmly suggest that you net your own fish. There is nothing worse than having your boat partner make a mess of netting a fish for you, particularly if it gets away. Not only does this lead to strained relationships, it also introduces an element of frustration into your own fishing. The same thing applies to your boatman, where appropriate. Let him hand you the net, spoon the fish afterwards, and put it in the bass bag. But unless your boatman is really first rate and wholly competent, you should do the job yourself.

That all-important first fish is in the boat – the smile tells all.

Captaincy

Another thing about boatmen concerns the 'captaincy' of the boat. Most days the rule will be two hours on and two off, with the angler in the stern having control. In the best possible circumstances, this should be friendly and relaxed, with most competitors favouring a joint decision over where to fish, whether to use the drogue, and so on. However, you should remember that the boatman is there to arbitrate if required, as well as to assist with the running of the boat.

Personally, I usually prefer to take the engine myself, rather than let the boat-man do the job. In this way, you go exactly where you want to go, and not where he thinks you mean, thus saving time and frustration. However, this does not apply to the loughs and lochs of Ireland and Scotland, where the local ghillies have immense skill and experience. They will know the waters intimately, and will be able to give immeasurable help and advice. At times like this you should simply defer, and stay firmly in the fishing seat while the boatman gets on with his job.

I experienced this myself at the Loch Leven International in 1987, when my boatman was a tremendous gentleman by the name of Dave Mancur. Things were

'The Gun' – all systems go!

relatively light in terms of fish caught, and despite Dave's best efforts to find the trout they were few and far between. When I did manage to hook one I reluctantly broke my own rule and accepted Dave's offer to net the fish. I need not have worried. Even before I thought the fish was beaten he had it out of the water with one deft sweep of his net, commenting 'No need to leave them in the water longer than necessary, Chris!' It was great stuff, and a treat to watch.

Timing

Finally, a tip about timing. Most matches finish at 6 p.m. and I have known more than one occasion when anglers have been disqualified for being late in getting back to base. There is really little excuse for this, as no matter how exciting the fishing might be you should always ensure that you are 'home' on time, especially if you have a catch to be weighed. It is far better to fish the last ten minutes in the relatively unlikely waters off the landing stage than to have your catch rejected due to a late arrival.

So much for generalisations. The real business of match day is about tactics, and how the individual angler interprets weather, fishing conditions, and the fishery itself.

6 Tactics

Loch style tactics are based on the best traditions and techniques of boat fishing on wild Scottish or Irish waters, which have been refined and improved upon over many generations to the extent where, with the benefit of modern tackle and technology, they have been elevated almost to an art form. It should therefore be made clear at the outset that there is much in loch style that defies definition – you cannot guarantee success merely by reading every article or book on the sub-ject, getting the best tackle that money can buy, and fishing the finest waters in the country.

However, whilst the skills of good fly fishing cannot be taught they can, thank-fully, be learned. This might sound like something of a paradox, but it is in fact quite true. You only have to look at the clean, fluid action of an experienced fly caster on the one hand, and a novice on the other. Like many skills in fly fishing casting has to be acquired, and hours of

No time for the 'fair weather fisherman'.

A good fish heads around the bows.

practice and self-teaching are involved.

In similar vein, I would suggest that there is little point in the newcomer to fly fishing entering any major competition until he has at least a few years of 'normal' sport under his belt. There really is no substitute for experience, and the most successful competition anglers, particularly those who are consistently successful, will have a vast reserve to call upon. It is one thing to become proficient on your local water, but quite another to handle venues as diverse as Rutland and Mask.

This is not meant to sound negative in any way, although I do accept that it is something of a 'Catch 22' situation. After all, how can you gain this vital experience without actually taking part? What I am saying is that loch style competitions are not for beginners to fly fishing, but for those who are already reasonably competent as anglers.

General Tactics

There are three fundamentally important questions to answer on a day afloat, and they apply to any day, competition or otherwise. Where are the fish, at what depth are they feeding, and on what are they feeding? Every single aspect of tactics and technique revolves around these factors, and everything that we do should reflect our interpretation of the answers to these questions.

It is for the individual to make his own assessment of the water on match day, and this usually begins with an anxious look at the weather as soon as he wakes in the morning. The decision on how to start the day's fishing is normally taken in the car park, although if conditions generally are close to practice day then preconceived plans will apply. Hopefully you will have a fair idea of where any concentrations of fish are – the so-called hotspots – and what line you will be using. However, an overnight weather change can throw things into great confusion, as this all too often results in a complete change in the fishing.

The one factor that can directly affect the answers to those three big questions is undoubtedly the weather. Rarely do we seem to be able to link a major competition with the elusive 'perfect' fishing day of high cloud, good ripple, and warm breeze. More often it seems that we have high gales and lashing rain, or bright steely skies and a flat calm. No matter; whatever the conditions all the anglers start equal, and it is up to each individual to tackle them as best he can – a point worth remembering when the going gets tough.

Floating Line Fishing

I always start the day with a floating line, unless there is absolute proof that this is wrong. Many years ago, my good friend John Braithwaite said to me 'always do what you know you do best'. This is sound advice, and if you are totally confident in your top-of-the-water technique it will normally serve you well, when in need of a yardstick. However, if icy winds are taking the tops off the waves, and there is no sight of a fish near the surface, then I will reluctantly adjust to a sinking line. Density and

Five fish before lunchtime is good in anyone's language.

sinking rate will obviously depend on the depth of the water being fished, or the expected depth at which fish can be found. Skilful use of a sinking line is a tactic in itself, and is discussed later in this chapter.

Short Lining

Short lining is probably the most traditional of all the loch style techniques, and when practised correctly is a joy to watch. In theory, it involves a short cast of perhaps ten or twelve yards, and working the flies back primarily by using the rod. In direct contrast to long lining, there is very little work done by the retrieving hand, and all the 'life' in the flies is imparted by the rod. This is probably the very essence of the dibbling technique. Too many people *think* they are dibbling, whereas in

effect they are only really slowing down the last few yards of the retrieve.

Real dibbling involves working the rod, sometimes at full arm's stretch, for upwards of half a minute. At such times you are not retrieving, but simply moving the flies in the waves, in all directions. This has a teasing effect on the fish, as well as giving a loose representation of drowning insect life in the water surface. If in doubt, just hold on to the dibble longer than you think is necessary, and you will be amazed at the results.

By definition, dibbling techniques need a longer than average rod, with the ideal length between ten and twelve feet. This is not to say that the same results cannot be achieved with a shorter rod, it's just that you will have to work very much harder.

To me, short lining is at the very heart of

Two fish in a flat calm.

loch style tactics, and yet so many anglers hardly explore its possibilities at all. The whole team of flies must be involved, not just the top dropper; they all have their part to play. The real advantage of short lining is that it can be employed in almost all weather conditions, from gentle ripple to high wave. When the fish are well up, and really moving, it can be a real match winner. If it has a disadvantage it is perhaps that it is a little inflexible.

Long Lining

If Bristol anglers have made any real contribution to the competition scene it is undoubtedly that they have exposed the real value of long lining. 'Fine and far off' is the way it is often described, and it has resulted in a string of major wins over a number of years.

Long lining is the most versatile of all stillwater techniques, and as such it is also the most demanding. Skilled exponents of the tactic will often use the entire length of the fly line with every cast, and yet they will need only one, or at the most two, false cast to lay that line on the water. For my own part, I find this a great advantage over any other method, with the benefit that it can be combined with so many other minor tactics. Frequently it gives the ability to cover fish at maximum range, and earlier than your boat partner. If the fish does not take at the first presentation of the fly, you still have time for a second

'When the going gets tough . . .'

or third cast, especially if fish are moving in a haphazard direction.

When using a long line technique you are not prevented from making short casts, and thus you have the best of both worlds. Dibbling and working the flies in the last ten yards is also part of the style. Long leaders can be used with ease, provided leader construction has been done properly.

Fish will be often more confident about taking a fly that is well away from the boat, and this is particularly relevant to calmer conditions. Trout can easily be spooked either by the boat, or by the line flash from short lining, whereas this does not apply when the fly is presented at long range.

Side Casting

Too many people have the view that loch style is simply about drifting downwind and casting and retrieving in front of the boat. If it were true, this would be monotonous at best, and intensely boring at worst. Thankfully it is not true, and the angler who explores all the options available to him will be in with a far greater chance of success. Each angler has a full 90 degree arc to play with, and under international and Benson & Hedges rules (which cover every event that matters), this means that fish rising well to the side of the boat can also be covered.

Side casting is a style for a windy day, or at the very least for a good ripple, as it actually uses the downwind movement of the boat as part of the retrieve. It has its obvious uses when fish are up and moving, in that a fly presented 'across the nose' is devastatingly attractive to feeding trout. But with less surface activity it is a way of moving flies across the wind to make them more visible, more lifelike, and therefore more appealing. You should vary your casting as much as possible, using as oblique an angle as you can comfortably manage, depending on the wind.

A variation on this particular theme involves the last fifteen yards or so of the retrieve. Given the movement of the boat, a cast made at 45 degrees to the central line will be coming back, at the end of the retrieve, at almost 90 degrees. With twelve to fifteen yards of line left on the water you can mend or throw the line downwind, resulting in an S-shaped retrieve pattern. It is a well-known fact that changes in direction of fly movement can prove very attractive to the trout, and this is a minor tactic I employ very often. It is particularly good when trying to tempt resident or experienced fish that have become fussy or selective in their feeding.

The glory of side casting is that it links in directly with long lining, thus forming a formidably effective double act. As always, vary the speed and style of retrieve as much as possible, with long, slow pulls interspersed with short six-inch jerks. If you have the age-old problem of fish that are following but will not take, despite the usual remedies of stopping, re-presenting, or speeding up, then a side cast may be the answer.

A Team of Flies

In fishless situations it is all too easy to slog on regardless, in the vain hope that the law of averages will work in your favour. Most of the time it won't, and you will be left changing flies *ad infinitum*. On the other hand, it pays to be able to recognise when things are going right, and to capitalise on it. There are, after all, times when the fish can't have too much of a good thing, and each rod's team of flies can be replaced with three or even four of the same pattern.

Many years ago I learned from Steve Pope, a Bristol angler of some note, that this can be phenomenally effective. It was Grenadier time at Chew, that wonderful period in early summer when fish are really 'on the top' and totally preoccupied with the big red midges. I had my own Grenadier on the top dropper, as did everyone else, but Steve's catch rate was quite amazing. Later discussion at the lodge revealed that, at the height of the action, he had changed his cast to *all* Grenadiers; no nymph on the point (which the fish weren't interested in), and no buzzer in the middle (which they didn't want either). Just three Grenadiers, as it was obvious this was what they *did* want.

The message here is obvious – if fish have fixed their feeding activity on one particular insect don't be afraid of offering them more than one chance of seeing yours. There is no point in offering them things they don't want on the odd chance that you might knock one off balance.

As ever, the converse is also true. If the trout are in a fussy mood you should use the full range in your team of flies, using all the logical possibilities in an attempt to find a fly, or combination of flies, that will work. Faced with a completely 'cold' practice day, with no visible fly life on the water, I will usually try a buzzer or small Hare's Ear on the top, a traditional or palmered fly in the middle, and a larger nymph on the point.

If it is possible to 'match the hatch' then you should do so, whilst remaining flexible. If sedges are everywhere try a Sedge Pupa on the point, Invicta in the middle, and maybe a greased Palmer at the top dropper, until the fish show a preference. That way you cover both the various stages in the insect's life cycle and varying depths of water.

The Single Fly

The single fly is a minor tactic for days when the trout are really fussy. When the fish are steadfastly refusing every offering there is little to lose by experimenting with such tactics, and the use of a single fly can give results. A lot of anglers feel reluctant to experiment too far on match day, and feel 'naked' without a team of at least three flies, believing they are adding to their chances with the extra patterns. Their anxiety is largely unfounded, as it must be fairly obvious that a taking fish is only interested in one fly at a time.

Indeed there is a strong case for single fly fishing, as there are definitely occasions when fish are put off by a team of flies and the attendant water disturbance caused by three or four flies landing on the surface. These exceptionally difficult situations are easy to identify: fish will follow, but not take; they will swirl at flies without actually striking; they will be feeding avidly, but will refuse all flies, no matter how well presented. In short, these will be occasions that are frustrating in the extreme, and I suggest that this is the time to try a single fly.

There is no mystique involved in using a single fly. Simply remove the droppers, use a lighter breaking strain nylon in the point section, and tie on a single buzzer if midges are hatching, or a suggestive pattern like a small Pheasant Tail or Hare's Ear Nymph if there is no strongly identifiable insect life

A fine winning basket at Leven.

The 'Rolling start' at Rutland.

Jockeying for position.

The vital process of fly selection.

Into a fine fish on Lough Mask.

The gin clear water of Avington.

Perfect drifting conditions.

Terry Oliver with an immaculate Leven brownie.

Peter Thomas takes the compulsory lunch break on Mask.

England's Brian Thomas displays his 'fishing sweater'.

around. Accurate and careful presentation, so much easier to achieve with a single fly, will often bring results.

Greased Line Fishing

Greased line fishing is another minor tactic for difficult fish or impossible situations. Conditions are much the same as for single fly fishing, but the time to grease-up is when the trout are taking food right in the surface film.

Trout that are preoccupied with surface film insects are almost oblivious to a fly presented at any depth – they simply ignore it. At times like these, a normal team of flies will be sinking just a few inches below the surface, and even these few inches are too many. The answer is to grease both the leader *and* the flies, probably the top two droppers on a three-fly cast. Any of the current brands of floatant will suffice, although the silicone gels are the best. To work properly the speed of retrieve should be slowed considerably, and again accurate casting is called for.

By far the best fly pattern for greased line fishing is the buzzer, in all its many variations. Typically, this insect is a victim of flat calm or near calm situations, where the pupae of the natural insects become trapped in the surface film, unable to break through to hatch. It is easy to see how this method is so effective, as the artificial flies are very realistic.

Because of the combination of circumstances it will be obvious that this is a tactic for the flat calms more than anything else, and is one of several ways of combating this most dreaded of angling situations. It is only secondary, though, to my own favourite antidote to a flat calm, the stillwater dry fly.

The Dry Fly

The use of a dry fly is the most under-rated aspect of competition loch style, and indeed of all stillwater fly fishing. For some strange reason it is often regarded as being solely a method for rivers and streams. Surely, though, a tactic that has proved itself for generations as an effective method of taking trout in running water should warrant more serious consideration on the lochs.

Consider the basic principles behind our stillwater sport. If you cast aside lures and attractors, the hard facts are that fish feed on natural flies. Take this one stage further, and whilst feeding from time to time on a host of different aquatic items, they will still tend to concentrate on the two most prolific species of midge and sedge. Our conventional flies will imitate other stages in the life cycle of those insects, so surely we should give the adult stage a chance as well, and use the right imitation – the dry fly.

The use of a dry fly requires close attention to the tippet, as a finer point than usual is needed. The leader rig for a dry fly, or the hedged-bet dry fly, is illustrated on page 51, and it is vital that you use as light a tippet as you can handle. My dry fly box leans heavily towards patterns that represent adult sedge or midge, although it is as relevant here as anywhere to 'match the hatch'.

Dry fly fishing is essentially slower and more relaxed than conventional nymphing techniques, and it may be this that discourages competition anglers from trying the method; they feel that it is not active enough, and that they are not trying hard enough. However, casting a small size 14 dry sedge into the path of a rising fish can be very effective indeed. The trick is not to strike too soon or too hard – a gentle lift is all that is required, and only after the fish has rolled over on the fly. Nor should you worry about small flies not being 'man' enough for big fish, as they often take a better hold than their larger size 10 counterparts. The dry fly tactic can be a competition winner in every way, as has been proved on more than one occasion.

The Wake Fly

The whole concept of fishing a wake fly is based on creating disturbance right in the surface film. This can be achieved at short range by dibbling, but equally by using an ultra-buoyant fly pattern at long range.

Wake flies of various descriptions have been used for many generations, and range from the heavily-palmered traditional patterns so favoured by the Irish, through to the modern Mini Muddlers. They have a great advantage in that they can be used in either calm or rough conditions, with long or short lining, and at any position on the cast. That said, there is an undoubted advantage in using a wake fly on the top dropper, where if fish do not take it directly it may well 'pull' fish on to other flies on the cast.

My whole fly fishing philosophy, whether for competitions or otherwise, is

The all-important weigh-in.

based on natural items in the trout's diet, and so it may seem contradictory that flies like the Baby Muddler form the greater part of my lure fishing. But the Muddler is something of an enigma, in that it can be tied or trimmed to suggest all sorts of insect outlines, and could even be said to loosely represent the confused outline of various hatching sedges. With that unique ability to produce a wake when retrieved it is an essential weapon in the armoury.

Bob Fly Fishing

It may appear that we have already covered the use of the bob fly, but the controlled use of the top dropper is far too important to simply gloss it over as being an inherent and integral part of loch style techniques because to many people it is the *only* technique.

By definition, top dropper work is all about top-of-the-water sport. It presupposes that a floating line is being used, and that fish are feeding on the surface. Happily, this is largely true of the water supply reservoirs in England and Wales, and also of the loughs of Ireland. For my part I would say that at least fifty per cent of all my fish come to the top dropper, so there is much more involved here than mere coincidence.

Spider or palmer patterns have been the first choice for top dropper spot for many generations. The successes of flies like the Bibio and Soldier Palmer are legendary, and they fully deserve their reputation. My own fly box includes flies tied with varying 'weights' of palmered hackle; by this I mean single hackles for days of gentle ripple, and at the other end of the scale those with four or even five hackles for use in a really big wave, or as wake flies.

When dibbling it is always the bob fly that breaks surface first, and as such it is often taken at the point of emerging. You should try to hold the top dropper in the surface film for as long as reasonably possible, moving it through and across the waves.

Light Leaders

Fish are not nearly as stupid as some people think, and even the humble stockie can prove to be very selective on occasions. It follows that a fine leader will make your fly more convincing to the trout, especially the smaller flies that you are likely to be using in competition. The only prerequisite is that you will need a much lighter rod than usual – the stiffer rods will result in too many 'smash takes', and breakages in the leader.

In the past I have used leaders as fine as 2lb breaking strain in major competitions. With a very soft rod the playing of fish on fine tippets is great fun, and in difficult conditions you can afford to spend the extra time needed before bringing the trout to net. Obviously I would not recommend fine lines for sunk line fishing, or for big wave days, as the benefits are negated by the conditions.

Induced Take

The induced take is another minor tactic that has been 'borrowed' from the chalk stream fraternity, where it has been an established part of nymph fishing for many years. Its use on still waters depends largely on the visual elements, and as such it needs near calm conditions.

It involves fishing the team of flies back to the boat, but stopping some ten yards away. The flies sink a little, and are then drawn smoothly into the final dibble and lift. What happens quite frequently is that fish will follow the early retrieve without taking, but will then take savagely on the lift. You need to watch for leader movement, or even the sub-surface flash of the fish; hence the accent on the visual side of things.

In flat calm conditions, when all elements of the retrieve can be slowed right down, the induced take can really come into its own. You can hold the flies until they are nearly vertical in the water, and the final lift can be really slow. But watch out for the takes, because on calm days the trout are heading straight for one place only – the bed of the lake.

Sunk Line Fishing

Until the spring of 1987 I had tended to be somewhat dismissive about the use of a sinking line, being fairly sure about the efficiency of a floater for almost every situation. However, having shared practice day boats for the World Fly Fishing Championship with real sunk line specialists like Bob Morey, Bob Church, and Brian Leadbetter, my eyes were well and truly opened. I also learned a whole new range of minor tactics, proving conclusively that you never stop learning at this game, even after 25 years in the sport. It also illustrates yet again how inventive modern competition anglers are, and how the whole scene is a breeding ground for innovative techniques.

There is a strong case for the serious competition angler to possess all densities of sinking line in his tackle bag, from Intermediate through to the 'Hi Speed Hi-D'.

Thus armed, he will be able to fish effectively through all viable depths at most competition venues. Perhaps more importantly, he will have the *option* of doing so, and if his boat partner is catching with a particular line he will be able to follow suit.

Intermediate Lines

These are the most recently introduced of all line densities, although judging by their instant success it is hard to understand why they took so long to come into being. Most Intermediates allow the angler to fish his flies at a controlled depth, ranging from just sub-surface to around four or five feet down. We thus have all the advantages of a floating line, but without the visual element. Because of this we are compelled to 'feel' for the takes, as with any other sinking line, and thus their application is limited. They are, however, a great boon on calmer days, as there is none of the surface skate associated with full floaters. They are also good news in high winds, as they permit the fishing of the flies in rather than over the waves.

Care is needed in selecting the make of line, as there are distinctly different sink rates. Some are little more than slow sinkers by another name, which is not really what the name Intermediate is intended to represent. The best advice is to go by recommendation rather than advertising.

Slow, Medium and Fast Sinkers

These are the true sinking lines, with the potential to fish flies at depths down to ten or twelve feet, more in certain wind conditions.

Four fish in the boat, according to the ghillie.

Care should be taken in that international rules specifically debar sinking lines that have any metal content – most notably lead-impregnated lines. This need not be a problem, as technology has advanced to the stage where manufacturers can produce plastic lines in densities that give comparable sink rates to their metal-based counterparts. The ranges currently available cover every possible contingency and allow the angler to match the sink rate with the speed of retrieve required for specific conditions, which is vitally important.

High Density Sinking Lines

These are the very fast sinkers that really take your flies down to the deeps. My own favourite has to be the 'Hi Speed Hi-D' from Scientific Anglers, which is a line used by almost all serious competition anglers. Even with a heavy wave and drifting boat, a long cast with this line will take your fly comfortably into fifteen feet of water, which is normally the maximum depth achievable in boat fishing. People may *think* that they are achieving more, but in reality the bow in the line prohibits effective fishing at much greater depths.

The one problem that nobody wants – engine failure on match day.

Sunk Line Tactics

Far from being a last resort or a tactic simply restricted to cold weather and deep-lying fish the use of a sunken line requires as much skill as does a floater. Various nuances of technique are available with a sinking line, and it is important that the competition angler recognises the viability of a sunk line situation.

Let us assume for a moment that it is practice day on an unknown lake, that there are no fish moving on the surface, and that two team members in a boat are looking for fish. The most logical approach is for them to use two sinking lines of contrasting densities. In this way they will both explore different depths of water and should, with luck, find the level at which the fish are feeding. However, simply finding this depth is not enough; you have to ensure that your flies stay at the correct level, and with varying wind conditions this is not always easy. This is because in a strong wind the boat will drift far more quickly than in a gentle breeze; by doing so it will restrict the depth to which the sinking line can sink, and consequently the effective fishing area.

It should be appreciated here that sinking lines generally sink in a bow shape, rather than a straight line, and that not all of the retrieve is viable in terms of actually fishing the flies. This particular characteristic of sunk line fishing is far more accentuated in a drifting boat than when fishing from anchor in normal conditions. To a certain extent there is less control over the swim of the fly, and consequently the angler will need to be far more alert to any takes. Even quite a heavy pull from a fish may feel soft as the bow in the line cushions the moment of contact.

Whilst I am a devotee of floating line fishing I am still prepared to admit that there are many occasions on which the use of a sunk line can be absolutely vital to competition success. In the golden year of 1987 I used it almost exclusively at the World Fly Fishing Championship on Rutland and Grafham, and later in that same year on Leven. These were contrasting situations, in that spring and cold water on the English lakes could not have been much further removed from the gentle autumnal fishing in Scotland, and yet all three venues required a sinking line to explore the depths. On Leven, for instance, it was necessary to find underwater ledges, trenches and holes that were obviously fish-holding areas. The flies had to be moved as slowly as possible, as the trout were relatively lethargic, and consequently a medium sink line was the best choice. Conversely, on Rutland high winds meant that the 'Hi-D' line was the only way of presenting flies at the correct depth for any length of time.

Many people regard the use of sinking lines as exclusively a lure fishing method, and they seem to think that only mini lures and attractors should be used. This could not be further from the truth as nymphs and many small buzzer patterns can be utilised to good effect. I have frequently spooned fish that have been caught at great depth and found them to be chock-full of midge pupae, proving conclusively that the sunk line and tiny fly combination most certainly has its place. Other useful sunk line flies for competition include the Stick Fly, Pheasant Tail Nymph, Ombudsman and the ubiquitous Hare's Ear. For the middle dropper I generally favour the brighter traditional patterns such as Dunkeld and Silver Invicta but, as ever, the fish should have the final word in fly selection, and discovering their preference will frequently be a process of elimination.

Hold and Draw

Otherwise known as the sink and draw method, this is an absolutely deadly minor tactic when using sinking lines. The line is cast well forward of the drifting boat, allowed to sink, and then retrieved until the last five or eight yards of line are left in the water. Then, as the name implies, the angler holds the flies almost motionless in the water. When this happens the line and flies sink further until they are near verti-

cal in the water. They are then drawn to the surface, either in one long movement, or in a series of jerky pulls, sometimes holding the flies again at a different depth.

This is a highly effective method of fishing different depths of water, and of presenting flies in a very enticing manner. When the takes come they are savage in the extreme, in many cases pulling the rod tip beneath the water's surface. Because of the vertical nature of the retrieve you will often find that a better hook-hold is obtained, either through the top lip or firmly in the scissors as the trout turns downward with the fly.

With the varying speed of the drift in different wind conditions it should be

The fish that took Ireland's Dick Willis into the individual WFFC final in 1987.

noted that this method is easier to practise in a gentle breeze rather than a full gale, but it can be successful in almost any conditions. It is in some respects rather like reverse dibbling in that the flies are being worked at some depth.

Static Takes

Although this is a very minor tactic, it is one worth bearing in mind for any competition. The sinking line is cast well out and frequently you will find that the trout will take 'on the drop'. No action is necessary on the part of the angler other than acute alertness. Such tactics, and indeed such fish, should be regarded as a bonus.

You should also remember that the use of a sinking line doesn't prevent you from casting at rising fish should you see them. The trout will often find a sinking fly even more attractive than one that is held in the surface, and casting at solitary rises can sometimes prove to be a match winner.

Buoyant-fly Fishing

This is a tactic that was pioneered on Queen Mother Reservoir at Datchet and is perhaps more suited to concrete bowl reservoirs than natural lochs. However, as a minor tactic it can have its place and is therefore worth inclusion. It involves using a sinking line and a relatively short leader, to which a single fly is attached. On Queen Mother Reservoir this fly would probably have been a 'booby' pattern. This rather doubtful-looking fly employs highly buoyant material tied-in at the head, usually in the form of exaggerated eyes. The material is so buoyant that when the line is drawn slowly along the bottom of the lake the fly will be swimming some

three or more feet above it.

For competition use a smaller fly such as a suspended buzzer pattern may be employed, and whilst I have had little personal success with the method I know that there are some anglers who swear by it. Because of the slow retrieve required it is essentially a tactic for calm or near calm conditions, and as it was developed specifically for bank fishing it has a limited application to the major competitions.

Ancillary Tactics

Hand or Reel?

I do not propose to enter into the age-old controversy of whether fish should be played from the hand or the reel; the matter is too subjective. However, I have to say that I always play fish by hand. I find that this is safer, gives more positive control, and can also be a lot quicker. This last point is especially relevant to competitions, and never more so than when good numbers of fish are being caught. You may also have noticed that many competitors dispense with the need to reel-in between drifts. They simply retrieve the line, and hold the rod clear of the boat whilst motoring; the line is then ready for an immediate cast, as soon as the motor has been killed.

Use of the Drogue

Not all competition venues have boats with drogues as a standard fitting and unless all boats are thus equipped the use of a drogue will probably not be allowed. In any event, the decision on whether to use it or not will be a joint one between the two competitors in any boat.

Rods in the air for safety; navigation around the landing stage is never easy.

In my opinion the drogue should be kept for extreme conditions of high wind and wave, and should be employed only when absolutely necessary, to slow the boat enough for anglers to keep in touch with their flies. Otherwise, it can be as much of a hindrance as a help. Someone has first to set the drogue, and then retrieve it at the end of the drift. In some cases, as with the short Rutland drogue, for example, it can cause the boat to drift unfairly in one direction. There is also the awful possibility of a fish becoming entangled in the thing whilst it is being played. Personally I prefer to let the boat drift freely, and in this way to cover more water.

Weight Loss

It has been proven that fish left in bright sunlight in the bottom of the boat can lose up to fifteen per cent bodyweight in an eight-hour period. Conversely, those fish kept in a cool, wet place lose little or no weight in the same period. Many competitions have been won or lost by mere ounces, so the message is clear – *always* use some form of bass bag, and keep your catch as cool and wet as you possibly can.

Reactions on the Take

Anyone who has fished on Lough Conn will know that lightning-fast reactions are needed to hook the rising fish. Unless the hook is set fast and firm the trout will be on its way back to the deeps. What is not so well know is that the opposite can sometimes be true, especially with fish taken on sunk line tactics. Some dour trout tend to take a lazy, slow hold on the fly, and reactions that are too fast will simply pull the fly away. I have seen Loch Leven ex-

perts barely tightening the line into a fish, and yet when they come to net they have the fly firmly in the scissors, as though perfectly set.

There can be no hard and fast rules here, but it pays to investigate the possibilities on practice day. If the fish are on top and moving fast, then reactions will be needed to match. But if they are slow and lazy, like those at Bewl, Leven, or Wimbleball, don't be afraid to slow things down accordingly. You sometimes need to 'reach for the take' as though removing china from a shelf!

Knots and Leader Quality

It is not generally known that some leader material responds better to certain knots than to others. This has much to do with the 'finish' on the nylon (matt or gloss), but it is also dependent on how good the angler is at tying the knot in question.

It still amazes me how many people rely on the out-dated Blood Knot for their droppers. The Water Knot, or grinner, is far better and more reliable. In the same way, the Clinch Knot is the only one to use for attaching the fly to the leader. Even when in a hurry always make sure that you moisten the wraps before pulling the knots tight, especially in the lighter diameters, as friction can weaken the finished knot.

Leader quality, and indeed brand or make, is a very subjective matter. The most expensive brands are not always the best, and it is for the individual to make his own choice. The new double strength varieties are good, but remember that what you gain in diameter you may lose in having excess 'shine'. It's a balancing act, and always will be.

Bob Williams, of Benson & Hedges, makes light of the weather.

Famous faces – Bob Draper.

A Final Word

So much for the quantifiable aspects of tactic and technique. They are easily understood, and with practice they will enable any competition angler to improve his catch rate and overall performance. But what about the indefinable 'something' that the top anglers possess? What special spark separates them from the rest, and why should they be so consistently successful? Is it, indeed, something that can be identified at all, or is it just the fact that they have a 'feel' for fishing that gives them such an edge?

The answer is almost as elusive as the question. Part of it has to be experience, for which there is little or no substitute. Another part has to do with good eyesight, which is an undoubted advantage in that the angler who can discern between a wave top falling in on itself and the rise of a trout will be the one who covers more fish. Keen vision is a major attribute, and one that is vital if all chances are to be taken.

Part of it also is about 'feel', both physically to determine the slightest touch of a fish on the fly, and mentally to be 'at one' with the lake and its surroundings. It has always been true that the best fishermen are those who are in tune with the countryside and its inhabitants, and this is never more so than with competitive fly fishing. The ability to read the water, to see beyond the hatching fly and think what may be happening at other stages in the life cycle, to almost think like a trout on occasions, these are the finer points that set the experts apart from the field.

In some ways, this approach is not something that can be learned or acquired. Rather, it is something that develops naturally, and in time. It cannot be purchased, but it can be nurtured, and applied to fishing in such a way as to increase one's overall capacity for the sport.

7 Running a Successful Team

Competitive fly fishing always has a certain 'edge' to it at whatever level, but never more so than when teamwork is involved. The ever-present fear of letting down your fellow anglers acts as a spur in itself, but even worse than that is the fear that a poor performance might affect next season's team selection.

From a team captain's point of view, the pressures are magnified tenfold. If a team is successful, he shares in their reflected glory. But if it fails, the long finger of accusation is pointed unerringly in his direction. The scapegoat mentality is alive and well, and as much a part of fly fishing as it is of cricket and football. The formation and running of a successful team is about a lot more than plain luck. It involves a whole range of things, from organisational work to man management and, on occasions, a very broad pair of shoulders.

The best illustration I can offer is inevitably centred upon my home team, the Bristol Reservoirs Fly Fishers Association. Around four years ago, whilst I was Honorary Secretary for the club, I was asked to form a team with a view to entering the Benson & Hedges tournament. It was a challenge in many ways. At that particular time the standing of the Association was shaky; relationships with the local Water Authority were strained, and several club members had been involved in some much-publicised misdemeanours. The formation of a successful team was seen as a chance to improve public awareness of our existence, improve relations with the fishery staff, and possibly to increase membership. Nobody could have had the slightest inkling as to how things would turn out.

Problems were not slow in showing themselves. To start with there were upwards of twenty candidates for a six-man team, and therefore some were destined for disappointment. There was, and still is, a great wealth of talent among Bristol fly fishermen, and forming a shortlist for the team was hard work. There were those who advocated some form of competition, but I firmly believed this to be counterproductive. Nothing is more important at club level than consistency, and results from our local competitions, as well as the known and proven ability of certain individuals, pointed the way.

I was also very aware that the chosen team would be flying the Bristol flag wherever they went, and as such would be acting as ambassadors for our club. Their success would reflect well on every Association member, at a time when credibility was very important. Above all we needed six individuals who would act as one team, both on and off the water. We almost needed to know each other's minds; we needed a total pooling of information, a sharing of ideas and theories, and a dedication to the team as a unit. Not everyone shared these views, however. There were those who felt that I should have chosen a mixture of floating and sunk-line specialists; others said that so-and-so warranted a team place because he had 'fished so well last week'. Advice, welcome or otherwise, was flowing in from all directions, and in great quantity!

In the event we made it to the Benson & Hedges final in our first year, finishing in second place behind Bob Draper's superstar team from the East Midlands, on their home water of Rutland. Not a bad performance by a West Country squad, and one which saw our club funds somewhat the richer. More importantly it also saw us considerably wiser, and more able to plan our attack for the following year.

Much of what followed is now well documented. The BRFFA have won the Benson & Hedges competition outright in 1986 and 1987, taking on all-comers from England, Scotland, Ireland and Wales. The essence of it all has been team-work, and a certain *esprit de corps* that is somehow beyond quantification. True, there is a great wealth of experience and ability in the team members, but beyond that they all genuinely believe in themselves, which I think is at the very root of their success.

I firmly believe that the best way of selecting a club team is to appoint a captain or manager, and let him select his choice, rather than holding some arbitrary competitive selection process. In any local club most people will know who the likely candidates are, and they will have proved themselves over a period of time. It's inevitable that some will feel that they are good enough, yet still not be selected but that should surely act as an incentive to further improvement.

Confidence is a key word in competitive angling, and each team member should feel sure and confident of his place, without the anxiety brought on by looking over his should all the time and wondering whether he will be 'dropped' at the next match. From a captain's point of view continuity is equally important, as he has to know how each man in his team will respond to different situations and water conditions.

The captain must also know the strengths and weaknesses of individual members. He must know who to allocate to a difficult spot for instance, or when to take the pressure off by giving another member his own freedom of choice. Some members might need psyching up, whilst others require no further stimulus at all. The competitive edge can be both good and bad, depending on the individual, and it is up to the captain to both recognise and capitalise on this.

We have been criticised in the past for taking our competitions almost *too* seriously, but I would refute this very strongly. True, we do our homework; I always hold a team meeting some weeks before the event, to discuss the water in question. We assess likely holding areas, sort out potential flies, and plan our practice day. On the eve of the match itself we will frequently be found tying flies at 11 p.m., especially if practice day has shown the fish to be preoccupied with a particular pattern. But these things are primarily done to increase the overall enjoyment of the event, rather than through any strict professionalism. The fact that such attention to detail pays dividends is just happy coincidence!

Perhaps above all else the team should be able to relax, sound in the knowledge that their captain has taken care of all the day to day matters. He should make sure that they are in the right place at the right time, that they have all checked in as directed, and that they know their boat numbers and allocations. With such mundane detail in the hands of the skipper, the team is free to concentrate on the more important aspects of preparation like setting up their tackle, and the vital process of fly selection.

The importance of getting the homework right cannot be over-stressed. On any practice day, a team captain should allocate areas of the water to his team in such a way that the whole lake is explored. I normally arrange for a lunch-break together, so that we can share our findings. In this way, individuals who have had a lean time in the morning will have the chance to cover a better spot in the afternoon, to try out their own thoughts on fly patterns, and above all to rekindle some confidence. Covering the whole lake is very important, as it's all too easy for the whole team to head for a known fish-holding area, completely neglecting 75 per cent of the water, only to find that on match day the fish have dispersed, leaving the anglers with no 'second string' to their bows, and without the faintest idea where to go.

A classic example of this kind of mistake was the 1986 B & H final at Grafham. All the homework pointed to the fish being fairly localised, and almost everyone headed for the same place. Everyone, that is, except one team. They had found a different concentration of fish that were relatively undisturbed, and they finished the day with a clear lead. In the evening it transpired that my team members who had been allocated to explore that particular area had not done so – they had seen fish moving in the more popular spot, and had just assumed it wasn't worthwhile. We made up ground on the second day, but it could just as easily have cost us the match.

Come the actual match day the captain's job is again a different one. By now he must have implicit faith and trust in his team, and must rely to a large degree on their performance. Whatever pressures exist for the team, they will surely be twice as bad for the skipper – thoughts of letting the team down with a blank are a veritable nightmare. Consequently, that vital first fish of the day is never more welcome, and once it's in the boat the captain can relax and enjoy himself.

During the match day team members will often pass each other in the course of changing areas, or between drifts. At such times, the team captain will try to build up a picture of how his team is doing, even though it will be largely guesswork. The match is never over until the final gun sounds, and one of the secrets of success is concentration, right up to the last cast.

Quite honestly there is no secret in either building or running a good team. The real job of captaincy involves total planning at every stage; this carries through to booking practice boats, hotels, transport, in fact everything that can make things run smoothly.

Whatever your motive for entering a competition the thing that really counts above all else is enjoyment – your own, and that of your fellow competitors. I would never select a team member who did not respect his fellow anglers, and if the subject of gamesmanship ever arose I would insist that a team member follows the simple courtesies of the boat. The friendships generated in all the major competitions are far too valuable to let a little thing like results get in the way. That said, the best way to a good result is good preparation. That all-important element of confidence begins with careful planning. What happens on the water is then, to a certain extent, in the lap of the gods.

8 A Day Out

No amount of carefully-descriptive prose can ever capture the real atmosphere of a major competition. Every day is different, every match unique, and every occasion special. But to try to paint some of the picture, let me take you now on a guided tour of one of the most hotly-contested matches of all – the English National. The date, Saturday 29 August 1987. The venue, Draycote Reservoir, near Rugby. Many hundreds of anglers from all over England had been fishing elimination matches since May, and now the final 64 had converged on this one spot to compete for the coveted top 20 places, and membership of the two England squads for 1988.

It was my second trip to Draycote, and the Midlands water held good memories for me. The previous occasion had also been a National final, and I had finished in third place after an entertaining day which had involved great top-of-the-water

Back to the landing stage, after the Chew International.

sport. Practice day had indicated that we might expect more of the same, so spirits were fairly high.

Match day always begins with an anxious look at the weather, and at the early hour of 6 a.m. we had been rewarded with the happy sight of very high cloud, and barely a breeze. Happy, because this meant that conditions would be more or less the same as practice day, and therefore our overnight decisions about floating line and small flies would still be appropriate.

My good friend and regular boat partner Martin Cairncross arrived at the car park with me, and our first sight of the water confirmed our expectations. Small feathery areas of ripple were interspersed with patches of flat calm, and there was no sign of any sustained breeze. Many people might have despaired at this, but our 'Bristol style' is well suited to handling such conditions, and so we were in no way dismayed.

We signed in, and then set about the careful process of preparation. As more and more anglers arrived the atmosphere slowly built up, until Brian Pargeter, the local organiser, gave us the final briefing on the landing stage with only ten minutes left until the gun at 10 a.m. I had been drawn with a local angler, Mike Ashley, who was to prove excellent company during the day. Because of a shortage of boatmen, we opted to go out on our own, as this gave us more space in the relatively small Draycote boats.

At the start Mike was happy to motor across to Biggin Bay, an area where we had seen most surface activity on practice day. It was also an area where there was at least a semblance of ripple, and as we started the first drift it was obvious that the trout were well up. Initially they were on the fussy side, rejecting our first-choice flies in an infuriating way. There were some small black midge on the water, yet all the obvious buzzers, Black Gnats, and slim Black and Peacock Spiders were ignored.

Mike took his first fish around 10.30 a.m., and his smile made me recall the words of Steve Pope many years earlier; 'The first fish is the only one that matters – after that it's all downhill.' How true! With a fish in the boat you are at least sure of a weigh-in.

Soon after this I had my own first fish, taken on a small Pheasant Tail, shortly followed by another to the same fly. We had drifted down to the corner of Biggin, by Lin Croft, and saw some fish moving out by 'E' buoy, another noted spot on practice day. Accordingly, we moved out beyond the buoy, and at this point I decided to scale down the leader size. Too many fish were following in but refusing the flies, and in near calm conditions the 4lb leader looked too big. I always feel better on light line, and no sooner had I changed to 2½lb than things started to happen. A long wind lane, or more accurately a wide band of calm water, stretched out towards Toft Bank, and there were rising fish everywhere.

In one drift I had seven fish, with Mike taking four. It was a fabulous first hour, and from the relative inaction in adjacent boats we were feeling fairly pleased with ourselves. Trout were snatching at tiny buzzer patterns, my favourite Soldier Palmer variant, and the Pheasant Tail. Mike was using similar flies, and also one of his own patterns which closely resembled a Palmer, but tied with a silver grey base. The best part of it all was that we were casting at individual rising fish, and this one-to-one contest is surely the very best of loch style fishing. Sport at its finest!

Exchange of views.

Ten fish by midday is a good bag in anyone's language, and with Mike following close behind as an extra spur, I was having a great time. Mike was terrific company, and we were constantly exchanging ideas as the day progressed. Conditions had hardly changed, and indeed they were to hold throughout the day as near calm. By 1 p.m. the trout were becoming very selective, and we had as many pulls and tweaks as we had fish. We could also see other boats losing fish, so it looked as though everyone was having similar problems. I tried slowing down the retrieve to near static, even when covering specific fish, and this was rewarded with two in quick succession. Then I entered my disaster patch.

Losing fish once hooked is never my favourite pastime, but when they come off at the net it is particularly galling. When this happens three times on the trot you start to doubt your own ability, and I was beginning to wonder if I was ever going to bring a fish to the boat. Almost incredibly, between 2 p.m. and 4 p.m. this happened ten times. Fish seemed to be taking the nymphs with confidence, but for some reason they just kept coming unstuck. Hook points were fine, I was playing them carefully, but they would not stay on. On the other hand Mike was having his 'purple patch' and could do no wrong. He was rapidly catching me up, and I was ruefully thinking of all the missed opportunities of the morning, when at least the hooked fish had stayed on.

But then, as often happens, things started to improve. I hooked a better than average fish and decided to play him hard, with nothing to lose. The trout had other

ideas, but after a spirited five minutes he was in the net, all 3lb of him. On a day when the average weight was around 1¼lb this fish counted as at least two, and possibly as three for the weigh-in. The fly responsible was a small size 14 Sedge Pupa, recommended by local expert Jeremy Herman, who had kindly agreed to act as ghillie for Martin Cairncross and myself on practice day.

We had stayed off Biggin Bay almost all day, displaying the angler's usual reluctance to leave a known fish-holding area. The last hour of competition saw fewer fish rising, and as we drifted a little further down towards Toft, we were rewarded with another fish apiece, both coming to

The author, just after losing a three pounder at Rutland.

Pheasant Tail nymphs fished well below the surface. We were still on floating lines, but by holding a near-static retrieve we were able to use heavier gauge hooks and allow them to sink to around four or five feet down. Thus, by using the stillwater-induced take we were taking fish sub-surface. The good news was that these fish took hard and with great confidence, resulting in a productive last hour for us both.

At the final tally I had 20 fish and Mike weighed in 16, easily the best boat of the day, and enough to give us first and second places. My fish weighed 28lb 6oz and Mike's 20lb 7oz, a real tribute to the sport at Draycote, and with the trout's hard-fighting qualities we were just as exhausted as we were fulfilled. It had been an ideal day, perfect in so many ways: the conditions had been difficult, but interesting; fish had been on the top, and catchable with the right flies; but above all the ambiance had been superb.

It looked as though Mike and I had qualified to fish the 1988 International in Conn together, and so we would have further opportunity to share ideas and theories. A great day, great company, and great fishing. Surely, nobody could ask more from his chosen sport.

9 The Fisheries

Perhaps one of the greatest benefits of being a serious competition angler is that you have the chance to fish at a large number of different venues. Each water has its own charm and individuality, and each provides its own challenge.

It can come as quite a shock to anglers who feel that they have mastered loch style techniques on their home water to find that an entirely different set of circumstances exists when they are 'playing away'. In many ways they will need to start completely from scratch, learning first about the water itself, and then about the most effective way of approaching it. As ever, the successful angler will be the one who can adapt most readily and who is able to leave all preconceptions behind him.

Every fisherman has his favourite water, and every venue has its own merits. There was recently a lobby, albeit a half-hearted one, to centralise all major competitions on one large reservoir, possibly at Rutland. Whilst I can see that this has some advantages, I am bound to disagree with the concept simply on the grounds that anglers would be missing out on the chance to fish the almost infinite variety of waters that exists in the British Isles. We should never deny ourselves an open mind and the great opportunities for learning that always occur when we fish a new water.

What follows, therefore, is a quick guided tour of the principal competition waters in use at the present time. Some have great reputations, whilst others are not so good. I have listed them country by country, but not otherwise in any particular order; neither have I gone into great detail with maps, favoured drifts, and the like. This is because such information is far too general to be of any specific value – the real work of assessing the water begins when anglers arrive at the lodge, and start to formulate opinions of their own.

Another reason for not going into too much detail is that the fisheries themselves will always be the best source of information (*see* Useful Addresses). I have found over the years that the people on the spot, whether they be individual owners or employees of vast water authorities, are incredibly kind and generous when it comes to providing help and advice. Far from being secretive and favouring their local team, they are completely non-partisan, and seem to want everyone to enjoy themselves in equal measure. It always pay to cultivate friendship with local ghillies, boatmen and fishery staff, as these are the people who will have the best up-to-the-minute information.

Scotland

Loch Leven

In any review of this nature it really would be impossible to start with any other fishery than Leven – the true home of

Australians and English share ideas on loch style.

competition fly fishing, the seat of learning for generations, and arguably one of the most picturesque of all waters.

The fishing is based around the town of Kinross in Perthshire, although at over 4,000 acres the extremities of the loch are well away from civilisation. It features two main islands, St Serf's and Castle, which make good reference points, as do the five smaller isles. Leven is essentially a shallow loch, with few areas of really deep water. This, coupled with the fact that you are fishing for essentially wild brown trout, means that almost all of the loch can be productive. There is little or no shoaling among the fish, and with such a vast expanse of water, they are naturally well dispersed. Re-stocking does take place, with native brown trout only, but by the time the fish take the fly they are as near wild as makes no matter.

Leven has had many ups and downs in its long history. Once famous for surface feeding fish, recent years have seen a significant increase in the use of sinking lines, with a good 'rise' being something of a rarity. Smaller flies seem to work well, with the most popular range being sizes 10 to 16 standard shank, which coincides happily with competition rules. Fish show

Bob Church, understandably happy.

a distinct preference for traditionals like Dunkeld; I was told by a veteran of the loch that I should 'never make up a cast that does not include a Dunkeld', and in two major matches that I fished there in 1987 this was sound advice. The teal feather flies like Peter Ross and Teal and Green also work well, as do Wickham's, Black Pennells, and Soldier Palmer. The Scots' own favourite, 'wee doubles', tied on tiny double hooks, are an undoubted help in hooking shy or recalcitrant fish holding in deep water.

To really confuse things, trout can be taken from right in the margins out to the very middle of the loch, and there are so many recommended drifts that it is impossible to list them all. A small booklet is available at the pier and this contains suggested drifts in all possible combinations of wind and weather. The wood clinker boats are superb – there is no bank fishing – and are rock steady in all but the strongest wind.

The best advice I can give is to suggest that you look carefully at the counter map on display at the lodge, and discuss the current trends with the fishery staff. Trout show a marked preference for holding in underwater trenches, shelves, and holes, and these need to be sought out and identified on practice days. As a rule of thumb, the more pressure on the water, the more it becomes necessary to use smaller flies; this worked particularly well in the tricky late summer Benson & Hedges final of 1987.

Leven is a beautiful place, with a mountain backdrop on all sides. It has an atmosphere all of its own, and is truly an experience to fish.

Lake of Menteith

Barely fourteen miles from Glasgow, Menteith is a 'lake' in the true sense, in fact the only one in Scotland. It was the decline in the fishing on Leven in the late 1960s that prompted the IFFA to look at Menteith, and the first International was fished there in 1971.

The natural head of browns is supplemented by stocking with rainbows, to the extent where it resembles the put-and-take style of southern waters. Very much so in fact, because at only 650 acres the lake is on the small side and consequently very manageable. In recent years many double figure rainbows have been taken, testifying to the richness of the water and the natural fly life.

Almost all the favoured reservoir fly patterns can have their day, with some locals showing preference for the silver-bodied traditionals, and heavily-palmered bob flies. The fishing seems to be better in early and late season, with a lot of surface activity making things ideal for loch style sport. Boats are glass fibre and sound, and as with Leven there is no bank fishing, allowing good free drifting in all areas. The average depth of the lake is around nineteen feet, and the best drifting areas are in Heronry Bay and Gateside Bay.

Loch Harray, Orkney

The Orkneys are another example of the wonderfully diverse and beautiful countryside that is enjoyed in the British Isles. The landscape is devoid of trees, but there is a wild, rugged and remote quality that leaves an indelible impression on the mind. Loch Harray epitomises this feeling, and a long drift down its shores, with not a living soul anywhere in sight, accentuates the solitude. Many species of birdlife inhabit Orkney, and the mournful call of wheeling curlews is one of the few sounds to intrude upon the fishing.

At 2,500 acres Harray is the largest freshwater loch on Orkney. It is also very shallow indeed, with an average depth of only 8 feet, and relatively few areas where the deeps exceed 14 feet. Vast patches of rocky shallows are the main feature, with great boulders rearing from below, and these areas provide ideal feeding conditions for the beautifully marked Harray brown trout, the fighting qualities of which are legendary.

All the traditional fly patterns work well here, supplemented by local favourites such as The Doobry, one of Stan Headley's best patterns. The Loch Ordie works well, as does the Wet Daddy and the long shank Worm Fly. In early season the fish tend to hold station nearer to the shores, whereas at the end of the year they will be found near the burn mouths, where they gather prior to spawning. There is also a run of sea trout in spring and autumn, coming in from Stenness.

All the local ghillies have their own favourite spots, but the truth is that fish can be found and caught all over the loch. They are free rising and very fast on the take, making for loch style sport at its best.

At the end of the day.

England

Kielder Water

Opened for fishing in 1982, Kielder is a relatively new water and as such has yet to gain any real prominence as a competition venue. It is only two miles from the Scottish border, making it one of England's most northerly lakes, and at nearly 2,700 acres it is also one of the largest, and is surounded by a vast man-made forest, with the trees almost standing in the water in places.

At the tail of Kielder is Bakethin Reservoir, constructed two years earlier than the main lake, and both hold a fair head of native brown trout, frequently supplemented by injections of stock fish.

The north east of England has not been too well served by top quality fishing venues, and the opening of Kielder should go some way towards reversing this. However, early fishing on the lake was disappointing, and this must be due in part to the acidity of the water, but it is also affected by the other recreational uses of the lake. Whether Kielder will ever challenge as a premier competition venue remains to be seen.

Rutland Water

Although I am a total devotee of the Bristol waters of Chew and Blagdon, if I had to choose one single competition venue above all others it would have to be Rutland. Right in the heart of England, and at the very centre of the immensely strong Midlands fly fishing scene, Rutland is just what a good loch style water should be: 3,700 acres of clean, clear water; mixed areas of deeps and shallows; prolific fly life; and a good mix of brown and rainbow trout. What more could we ask for?

If there is a problem at Rutland for the competition angler it has only to do with the size and shape of the place. It takes nearly a full hour to motor from the South Arm to the tip of the North, and this means that once you have selected your spot for the day, you are committed – it is simply not practical to waste an hour's fishing time for the long move. Consequently, practice day on Rutland is more important than anywhere else, as you need to find the fish, and feel confident that your choice is the right one.

Fish are stocked regularly throughout the season and are normally in excellent condition. Those that are not caught in the first few weeks after stocking will quickly gain weight, and tend to run to the shallower extremities of the two arms. Here they become semi-resident fish, and are well worth seeking out. If the going is tough, with relatively few fish being caught, then three good fish from Brown's Island will invariably weigh more than seven or eight stockies from the dam.

Rutland opened for fishing in 1976, and since then it has very quickly matured into a very beautiful lake indeed. The long Hambleton peninsula effectively splits the water in two, and provides a host of bays and creeks to add extra interest to the fishing. The famous Normanton Church, standing with its feet in the water, is a great landmark, and almost all of that bank right down to Berrybutts will offer good drifting. I have to admit to a preference for the South Arm, as the scenery is particularly good. Old Hall stands watch over the fishing, and there is no doubt that some of Rutland's better brown trout can be found here.

Rutland becalmed – Normanton Church in the background.

The lake is fickle, though, and there will not always be surface feeding fish around. You will therefore need the full armoury of floating and sinking lines, and you have to be prepared to use them all in any one day's competition. Most of the popular fly patterns work well, with the fish showing a distinct liking for Soldier Palmer, Grenadier, and many of the patterns incorporating reds in their colour scheme. I have been particularly successful on Rutland with small flies, in sizes 12 and 14, and even occasionally with 16s. In the gin clear water small flies and light leaders are a must, particularly in gentle conditions.

Fishing Rutland is not unduly compli-cated. The trick is not to let the vast size of the place put you off, as it can be a bit daunting at first sight. You really need to treat it as a whole series of separate fisheries, each with its own character. Once you know your way around, it is a fantastic place to fish.

Grafham

Grafham Water is a man-made reservoir, and in 1966 it was one of the first of a 'new breed' of fisheries to open for business. The early bonanza of huge fish in great numbers gradually settled down to a more consistent pattern of sport, and Grafham

93

A rough landing at Grafham.

today is one of the premier competition waters in England.

At roughly 1,600 acres Grafham is arguably the ideal size as a competition venue. It offers a good mix of open water drifting, with bays of various sizes, and a nice combination of deep and shallow water. The scenery is not as pretty as at Rutland, but the surrounding countryside consists of gently rolling farmland, providing at times a lot of terrestrial insect life on which the trout feed. In early autumn, when the 'Daddies' are on the water, there is some of the best possible sport to be had on the dry and dapping methods.

Without a doubt, smaller fly patterns work well at Grafham, and size 14s will be in frequent use. All the traditional patterns are good here, with small palmers being among the favourites. Wickham's, Invicta, and Grenadier have also taken large baskets for me in recent competitions.

Grafham is usually navigated via the fixed buoys, which help anglers find the fish-holding areas. Famous buoys like S-mark (off Savages) and G-mark (down by the dam) are known holding areas. Just off Church Bay is the 'spider tower', a pylon that leans drunkenly in the water after the ravages of wind and waves – it is great fishing here in early season. Again, the whole lake can be productive at different times of year, and a good deal of exploration is required to get things right. A practice day is virtually compulsory.

Draycote

I have some fond memories of Draycote, having fished there in two National finals, finishing in third and first places. It falls a long way short of being the most picturesque of reservoirs, but makes up for this by providing consistent top-of-the-water sport throughout the season. For this reason Draycote was a popular venue for the IFFA International in 1981, when large numbers of fish were taken.

To be frank, Draycote is mostly about stockie fishing, with relatively few resident fish available. It is small in comparison with most venues at only 600-odd acres, although this contains its own advantages in that no part of the reservoir can be deemed too 'remote' to warrant consideration. Nothing is ever too far away on Draycote, and you can easily keep in touch with what is going on in other boats, with no one being able to get too far ahead in the competition without other anglers realising what is going on.

Basically, Draycote is the archetypal put-and-take water. The recently introduced fish tend to be free rising and well dispersed around the lake. Even so, they can be infuriatingly selective at times, refusing all the standard offerings and demanding the subtlest of techniques to deceive them.

There is a good variety of water depth, with some shallow areas where fly life abounds, particularly the Toft Shallows. Prevailing winds mean that you can set the boat up for some long drifts along the productive banks, where the usual fly patterns for stocked rainbow trout will work

their way. My own preference for Draycote leans heavily towards small Pheasant Tail nymphs, teamed up with Grenadiers, Mini Muddlers, and Wickham's. Biggin Bay through to Cornfield and Toft is my favourite drift.

Bewl Water

Formerly known as Bewl Bridge Reservoir, this is a truly beautiful lake, set in the rolling Kent countryside just south of Tunbridge Wells. It is a big lake, and with a wealth of bays, creeks and quiet corners Bewl is an ideal competition venue with no end of possibilities for the fisherman.

The lodge is more or less centrally sited, with the dam to left, and two long straits to either side. Because of its configuration there are rarely occasions when strong winds can spoil the fishing. Conversely, there are so many good drifts on Bewl that it is almost impossible to choose the best spots; sport is consistent all over the lake. Hook Straight, with its many small bays, offers wonderfully scenic fishing, and 'the Nose' is also very popular. At the other end of the lake the intimacy of Dunster's Bay is appealing, as is the long, tight drift into Goose Creek.

The main feature of Bewl has to be the glorious countryside. You can see oast houses on the horizon, and much of the bankside is tree-lined. This last point is doubly significant, as it precludes bank anglers from fishing many areas, thus allowing the boats to drift close in – often essential in the relatively deep water. The rolling hills of Kent provide a perfect backdrop to the fishing, and Bewl has quickly become a favourite venue for anglers and spectators alike.

Tactics vary through the season, and

can change almost as dramatically as the weather. Basically, the conventional loch style techniques will suffice, with a strong leaning towards top-of-the-water methods. Because the lake is so deep it can take longer to warm up in the spring, and you should be prepared to use fast sinking lines in May competitions. Water quality is good, and there are vast banks of Canadian pond weed, much favoured by the trout. I have had a lot of success at Bewl with fine leader tactics, especially because of the great clarity of the water, but you should watch out for the occasional big fish when fishing very fine – Bewl has a good head of resident browns, and these fight long and hard.

Chew Valley Lake

I suppose it is inevitable that my home water should be my favourite, but even allowing for this it would be hard to imagine a water better suited to competitive fly fishing than Chew. At just over 1,200 acres Chew is big enough for all the major competitions, and the quality of its fish and fishing is known the world over.

Part of the reason for its huge success has to be the fact that the Bristol Waterworks rear all their own trout, in an elaborate hatchery that dates back to the turn of the century. The accent is placed totally on 'quality control', and the superb browns and rainbows are perfect fish, full finned,

Waiting for the 'off' at Chew. The National of 1978.

and great fighters. In particular the browns, which are only stocked once a year, are almost wild. Placed in the lake in January they put on weight rapidly, and represent a great challenge to the angler. In recent years a policy of augmenting normal stockings with fingerling fish has meant that there is a great build-up of resident trout.

Another reason for Chew's popularity is that it is fairly shallow, with an average depth of only 14 feet. As a consequence fish are often on the top, and in summer you will encounter rising fish all through the day, given favourable conditions. Because of this most Chew regulars will start each day with floating lines, regardless of the weather. Their confidence is rarely misplaced, and I would estimate that at least 90 per cent of my Chew fish come to the floating line.

Favourite drifts are over the Roman Shallows, off Wick Green, across Herons Green, and over the False Island. These are all shallow water drifts, and would be my first choice in May, June and July. Later in the season it can pay to look for deeper areas, and fish can be found near Nunnery, Woodford, and along the north shore. The dam area warrants serious consideration in hot weather, particularly if the aerators are in operation.

The fly life on Chew is prolific, so the accent is firmly placed on imitative patterns. The infamous Grenadier is found throughout the summer, with a heavy concentration in June, and is one fly that should always be on your cast on Chew. Other popular favourites are Wickham's, Invicta, Hare's Ear Nymph, Pheasant Tail – in fact the whole range of traditionals.

Water quality is excellent, and comes from a host of feeder streams from the surrounding Mendip countryside. Because of its clarity, especially in early season, fine leaders may be needed. This is never more relevant than in the dreaded flat calms, of which Chew seems to have more than its fair share. In such conditions a small Dry Sedge pattern, tied with Squirrel Tail wings (clipped) can work wonders.

To me, Chew is the classic loch style venue. It has everything that the discerning angler could wish for, and a whole lot more besides. The cream of the sport is undoubtedly in early and mid-summer, but this is very much an all-year-round lake, fully deserving of its great reputation.

Wimbleball

Wimbleball is the chosen venue for the Benson & Hedges heats in the south west of England. It is a relatively new water, but has matured very quickly into a natural setting. On the edge of Exmoor, and at fairly high altitude, it takes a long time for the water to warm up in spring, and with some very deep areas the fishing is testing.

This is another lake that is full of bays and creeks, all of which repay a little exploration. The general area of the sailing club bay is good, but most anglers prefer the wonderful scenery of Cow Moor, Bessom's, or the Upton arm. With no intrusion from the sound of cars or trains, the only noises will be the overhead cry of the buzzards, and the constant chatter of the migrant warblers. This is, indeed, a lovely place, and I have been lucky enough before now to see deer in the surrounding woodland, and a distant fox trotting over the moor.

In early season sunk lines and black flies are the order, with the local preference

The lull before the storm.

being for a Viva, or similar mini-lures. Darker Stick flies have also worked for me, along with Black and Peacock Spider, and Zulu. On days when the fish are up, Grenadier and Soldier Palmers are highly effective, with a Dunkeld as middle fly.

Wimbleball is not large, but it is intimate in a special way. There is enough room to get lost from your fellow anglers, and every chance of finding a fish-holding spot that can win you the competition. A practice day here is essential – and very enjoyable!

Wales

Trawsfynydd

Universally known and referred to as 'Traws', this has been the principal Welsh venue for the Home International series for many years.

However, with all the charity in the world, I cannot bring myself to be overly enthusiastic about Traws. A nuclear power station stands rather ominously in the centre of the scenery, and uses the lake's water in its cooling system. As a consequence the water is warm in spring, and positively hot in summer, which is hardly conducive to good fishing.

Fly life is sparse, the water very peaty, and the stock fish of indifferent quality. When introduced into the lake they are either caught quickly or seem to just disappear; there are very few resident fish at all. Couple this with the fact that bait fishing is allowed from the banks, and you can hardly wax lyrical about angling quality. Flies are fairly conventional, with a marked preference for black: Connemara Black, Zulu, Bibio, and Black Pennell are all popular, with Dunkeld, Butcher and Peter Ross for the brighter days.

Against its disadvantages, the social side at Traws is super, with all the teams staying in a holiday complex centred around a 'village' of log cabins. All the evening functions are held in one hotel, and the atmosphere is ideal.

More recently, Wales has been testing reactions by holding the IFFA International at Brenig, which is a better venue altogether. There is certainly more fly life, and consequently a better chance of sport.

Llandegfedd

Not yet a fully 'International' venue, Llandegfedd is nevertheless a worthy contender as host for the Welsh IFFA meetings, as was proved by the excellent results at the Youth Internationals in 1985. Set in the very pleasant countryside of the Usk valley, and with a good head of free-moving fish, Llandegfedd has much to recommend it. A good variety of water depth, interesting bank configuration, and prolific fly life all make for interesting fishing.

The local club scene here is as strong as anywhere in Wales, and I for one hope that this lake will be given the chance to prove itself that it obviously deserves.

Ireland

Lough Conn

Ask competition fly fishers about their ambitions, and a large percentage will surely answer that they would like to fish the queen of Irish loughs, Lough Conn in County Mayo. The reputation of Conn is truly international, and the myths and legends that surround it merely add to the overall appeal of the place.

The sheer size of Conn is daunting, with distances measured in miles rather than acres. There are many islands, and many areas of shallows, all of which hold fish. The vastness of the lough means that boats disperse themselves far and wide, with only very occasional bunching in known hotspots. As ever in Ireland so much will depend on your ghillie, without whose local knowledge you will be virtually lost. Not only can these magicians navigate their boats through the rock-strewn shallows, but they also have a kind of sixth sense when it comes to locating the trout. By far the best advice is to take a bottle of something with you, pour a dram at the outset of the day, and listen carefully to your ghillie – this is the most important tactic of all in Ireland.

Long drifts are possible on Conn, and in all but the lightest of winds there will be a good wave. The fish are much faster here than anywhere else, and lightning reactions are needed on the strike if you are to hook them. So often on Conn you hear people telling tales of countless opportunities in a day out, yet returning with only a fish or two in the boat. The fishing is very visual, and eyesight can play a greater part here than at many other venues.

The classic mayfly hatch is a feature of

The start at Melvin.

Conn, and if you are lucky enough to qualify for the IFFA Spring International you may have the opportunity to sample this superlative sport. Unfortunately, you can just as easily pick a day of high wind or gales, when fishing is uncomfortable at best, and downright dangerous at worst. Many locals stick to wet fly tactics on sunk line, with popular patterns including the Golden Olive, Black Pennell, and the ubiquitous Green Peter. Invicta, and Mallard and Claret should also be considered as essential.

Nothing can ever prepare you for the magic of Conn, and to fish an International there is an unforgettable experience.

Lough Sheelin

Because of its reputation, Conn is universally regarded as the centre of Irish fishing. Coupled with Lough Mask, which stages the annual 'World Cup' at Ballinrobe, these are probably the first two names that spring to mind in any discussions about Irish fly fishing competitions. But Sheelin, a 4,500 acre lough administered by the Central Fisheries Board, also has its place. It is only an 'occasional' International venue, and yet it can be infinitely more productive than the two big names. Fishing can be patchy through the year, but when Sheelin is 'on song' the trout can be plentiful, and hard fighting. Here again, the best advice is to take yourself to the local pub, buy a drink for the first ghillie you meet – and listen!

10 The Flies

By now it must be obvious that there is no such thing as a 'golden' fly, or flies. There is no secret weapon in my fly box, nor in any other competition angler's of my acquaintance. Conditions vary so much from day to day, from one water to another, and from one season to the next, that fly choice remains something of a permanent mystery, and a relative gamble. On the other hand, every angler has his own favourite flies, without which he would not dream of going fishing. And because he has confidence in the flies, and feels happy using them, he will probably catch more fish on those patterns.

However, the attentive reader cannot fail to have noticed that there are some patterns whose names have been repeated throughout the pages of this book, and are obviously successful on a range of different waters. Because of this, I have decided to provide a breakdown of what I consider to be good flies in the hope that this will make things easier for you to compile your own shortlist. All the patterns are well known, and you should have no trouble in either buying them at your local tackle dealer, or in tying your own. We are all faced with a baffling array of flies to choose from, and this list actually represents only a tiny fraction of the vast numbers of patterns that are currently available.

I see little point in going over the full dressings for all these patterns, as this has been done so many times before and by authors of much greater competence than myself. But I have given the dressings of some of my own flies, as well as some useful variations on established themes. Armed with this collection, or at least the best part of it, you will be well prepared for the vast majority of circumstances, on most of the competition venues currently in use.

For those anglers who prefer to tie their own, a word is needed here about hooks. It should be patently obvious that you should use the best quality hooks that money can buy, in *all* your fishing. When you consider the time spent in fly tying, the hours devoted to persuading a fish to take the finished product, and the importance of every fish at a competition weigh-in, then it is nothing short of absurd to use lower quality hooks. Tremendous grief is caused by losing a fish through hook failure, so please do not be tempted to cut corners: use a top quality British product like Partridge, and in some patterns use the brilliantly sharp Drennan range. The hook sizes I prefer are given, with less popular sizes in brackets.

Essentials

This list includes patterns that should feature in every competitive angler's selection. They are well proven, and have stood the test of time – and trout – for many years.

Wet Flies	Hook Sizes
Grenadier	10–14 (16)
Soldier Palmer	10–14 (16–18)
Mallard and Claret	10–14 (16)
Invicta	10–14 (16)
Silver Invicta	10–14
Connemara Black	10–14
Bibio	10–16 (18)
Zulu	10–14
Stick Fly	10–12
Stick Fly – Green Tag	14–16 (long shank)
Wickham's	10–14 (16)
Pheasant Tail Nymph	10–14 (16–18)
Mini Muddlers (various colours)	10–12
Peter Ross	10–14
Dunkeld	10–14 (16)
Black and Peacock Spider	10–16 (18)
Hare's Ear Nymph	10–16 (18)
Buzzers (various colours)	10–16 (18)

Dry Flies	Hook Sizes
Adult Sedge	12–16
Silver Sedge	12–14
Spent Midge	12–16 (18)
Cinnamon Sedge	12–16
Black Gnat	12–16 (18)
Daddy-long-legs	10–14
Mayfly (for Conn)	10–12

Highly Recommended

This grouping, whilst not as fundamentally essential as the first, still have much to recommend them, and certainly almost all these patterns will feature in my own fly box.

	Hook Sizes
Teal, Blue and Silver	10–12
Teal and Green	10–12
Wingless Wickham's	10–12
Ombudsman	12–14 (long shank)
Bumble	10–12
Viva	10–12
Mini Lures (black, white)	10–12
Black Pennell	10–14
Doobry	10–12
Butcher	10–12
Persuader	10–12
Green Nymph	10–12
Damsel Nymph	12–14 (long shank)

Specials

This group consists of a few of my personal favourites, both variations on established themes and my own dressings.

Green Nymph
Hook: Partridge code J1A, size 10–14.
Tail: Green hackle fibres.
Body: Light olive seal's fur, over-rib with fine copper wire.
Thorax: Dark olive seal's fur, with pheasant-tail wing cases over.
Throat hackle: Green hackle fibres.

Blagdon Buzzer
Hook: Patridge Captain Hamilton, size 10–16.
Body: Claret seal's fur – over-rib with fine silver wire.
Thorax: Peacock herl, with one turn of fluorescent red wool behind.
Wing case: Pheasant-tail fibres.

Grousewing Sedge (dry)
Hook: Partridge Captain Hamilton dry fly, size 10–14.
Body: Pheasant-tail fibre.
Wing: Natural grey squirrel tail, clipped to shape.
Hackle: Light brown cock.

Wood Duck and White
Hook: Partridge code G3A, size 10–12.
Tail: Pinch white hackle fibres.
Body: White ostrich herl, over-rib with fine silver wire.
Throat: Pinch white hackle fibres.
Wing: Wood duck (or strongly barred teal).

Heron Herl Buzzer
Hook: Partridge Captain Hamilton, size 12–16.
Body: Grey heron herl (or goose herl substitute).
Rib: Fine silver wire.
Thorax: Peacock herl. Pheasant-tail wing case over.
Breathers: White hackle fibre, tied in 'bow tie' fashion.

Green Grenadier
Hook: Partridge Captain Hamilton, size 12.
Body: Olive seal's fur (light).
Rib: Copper tinsel.
Hackle: Badger.

I am an absolute sucker for a big fly box. I spend many winter hours devising new flies, or making variations on established favourites, in the hope that one day I will discover something extra special. In truth, you can never have too many flies, and the angler who is prepared to experiment, and who has an open mind to both his fishing and fly design, will be in with a greater chance of success.

11 The Future

There are many factors likely to affect the future of fly fishing. Without a doubt, the growth of interest in the sport will continue, as witnessed by the proliferation of smaller regional competitions in recent years. The strength of the international scene has never been greater, with ever more individuals looking to qualify to fish for their country. When the Benson & Hedges tournament was first launched just 300 teams entered the fray. In the space of four years this grew to over 700 teams – a measure both of the competition's status and of the vast upsurge of interest among the participants.

Inevitably there are, and will be, those who seek to 'knock' the competition scene, as it appears to cut across their ideas of how the sport should be conducted. Much of the criticism comes from ignorance; therefore, those of us within the sport should always seek to educate and inform whenever possible. Anyone who has attended a World Fly Fishing Cham-

Synchronising watches – Benson & Hedges.

pionship would surely have been impressed by the great spirit of international friendship and unique atmosphere that pervades the whole event.

Every sport has it critics, and it is only by refuting any detrimental comments that it survives and grows. The way in which we counter criticism must be authoritative, convincing and accurate. We have associations and confederations who are easily capable of issuing guidelines to every member angler, to ensure that we all speak with a united voice. This solidarity within our own ranks is most important: nothing saddens me more than to hear fellow anglers giving derogatory interviews against competitive fishermen, as this gives a false impression of disunity to our opposers.

'Catch and Release'

There is at present a strong lobby from anti-bloodsport groups, who seem intent on curbing something that has always been a traditional part of country life. To resist this pressure all followers of field sports should unite to protect our right to hunt, shoot and fish. It therefore behoves us to take great care whenever fishing: leave no litter, discard no nylon casts, and dispatch your quarry cleanly and humanely. Indeed, when 'under the camera' we need to be even more careful. Allow your photograph to be taken by all means, but only show the photograher your best single fish, rather than a heap of corpses. Photographs of leering anglers above piles of dead trout do little to promote our cause.

Because of these problems, and because many sponsors are as concerned about their own image as they are for the actual sponsorship, the sport could well be moving towards a catch and release policy in major competitions. I know that this is a contentious issue, but it is a policy that works well elsewhere in the world, where results are decided on numbers of fish, rather than total weight. A combination of both is practised in America, where each fish caught is measured quickly by the ghillie, and then returned; there are points awarded for each fish, and then a standard scale of length against weight is applied. This can be remarkably fair, and would seem to be totally workable.

A catch and release policy would open up huge possibilities for competitive fly fishing. One of the main reasons for the lack of television coverage is the fact that the sight of a large angler bludgeoning a small fish to death is not attractive to many viewers. But if the art and skill of fly fishing could be conveyed, and if we could show that *points* rather than dead fish were the deciding factor in the results, attitudes would quickly change. Even on vast expanses of water like Rutland it would be perfectly possible for boat-borne cameras to home-in on the action. Smaller, intimate venues like Avington or Dever Springs would conceivably lend themselves to spectators on the day – something that is not currently encouraged.

River Venues

The advantages of including more river venues on the competition scene were clearly demonstrated in 1987 when the WFFC came to the River Test to decide the individual champion. The choice of water was ideal, and with a reasonable draw system to ensure that all anglers fished a selection of beats, I believe competitors welcomed the move. If the intention of any match is to prove the skill and versatility of the angler then surely it is relevant that he should be able to demonstrate such skills on both still *and* running water.

Sponsorship

I do not necessarily believe that the introduction of big money sponsorship would be as detrimental as some people think. Almost inevitably there are stars in this sport as in any other, anglers who are consistently successful and who can be relied upon for at least an above-average performance in any match. It would therefore seem a logical step to introduce a seeding system, so that the top names are not required to go through the prolonged process of elimination matches that presently exists. Apart from being a sensible step this would also win approval from the sponsors, who obviously like to have the big names in their tournaments.

To stay at the top of their sport these big names have to spend quite large sums of money to attend enough matches to maintain their prominence. This is perhaps where more sponsorship money would be appropriate. Unlike other sports, where representing your country costs little or nothing, top anglers who fish, for instance, two IFFA Internationals in a year, plus the various Benson & Hedges rounds, plus the eliminators and National, can quite easily run up high bills. Many anglers feel that there are sponsors 'in the wings' who would help greatly with these costs, and who are only waiting for the next opening to present itself.

John Sautelle snr. One of the real 'characters' of the WFFC in 1987.

Young and Old

One of the most encouraging signs for the future of the sport must be the great flurry of interest in the youth match scene. True progression in the sport requires a strong element of enthusiasm in younger anglers, and the fact that they can now graduate through from a fully-fledged Youth International is all to the good. At club and local level help is available for youngsters wishing to enter the competitive scene, and it is heartening to note that such help invariably comes from senior international anglers.

At the other end of the scale it is interesting to see that the age range of competitors is a wide one. At my first International in 1982 the oldest competitor was Bristol's Stan Pope, representing his coun-

The author discusses tactics at Avington with his ghillie, Chris Howitt.

try at the tender age of eighty! Older competitors bring with them a vast range of experience, and their anecdotes and advice make a delightful contribution to the proceedings.

A Final Word

With care, the future for competitive fly fishing is bright. However, it needs an input from all of us, in that we need to nurture our public image and standing. I firmly believe that we should pursue the visual side of things, to make the sport more exciting and entertaining for the serious spectator, and that in some respects we should promote ourselves more as sportsmen. In that way, more anglers would join our ranks, thus adding ever greater strength. I accept that we will never have the kind of crowds seen at Wembley, but I do believe that one day soon we may have the kind of interest that generates the numbers of spectators seen at coarse fishing matches. Such a development, and the corresponding increase of benefits to our sponsors, may hold the key to some real progress. Britain has been the home of fly fishing for many generations; with luck and hard work it will continue to pioneer the principal developments in the sport.

I sincerely hope that this book will have kindled a new interest in fly fishermen who have yet to try competitive angling. Similarly, I hope that by sharing some ideas and theories I will encourage those who have just taken up the sport. Some of the tactics described are rudimentary, others are advanced; either way, all can be exploited by the individual, and turned into part of his own special style. Fishing is, and always will be, a matter of personal interpretation.

I know of no other sport that offers the level of excitement and enjoyment that we have in fly fishing. In a way, we are indulging our age-old hunting instincts, turning them into an art form as well as a sport. We are, moreover, fortunate to enjoy fishing in fresh air, with the added advantage of beautiful scenery and surroundings. We also have the opportunity to share convivial and like-minded company for, as Izaak Walton sagely remarked, we are all 'brothers of the angle'.

In the final analysis, competitive fly fishing comes down to a man, with a rod and fly, in search of a trout. In this respect, nothing has changed in countless generations, and I hope it never will.

Useful Addresses

Scotland

Loch Leven
Loch Leven Fisheries
The Pier
Kinross
Perthshire
Tel   0577 63407

Lake of Menteith
Lake of Menteith
Port-of-Menteith
Stirling
Tel   087 75 253

Loch Harray, Orkney
Orkney Angling Service
Stymilders Finstown
Orkney
Scotland
Tel   0856 76306

The Merkister Hotel
Harray
Orkney
Scotland
Tel   085 677 366

England

Kielder Water
The Fishing Lodge
Matthews Linn
Kielder Water
Hexham
Northumberland
Tel   0660 40398

Rutland Water
Rutland Water Fishing Lodge
Whitwell
Oakham
Leicestershire
Tel   078086 321

Grafham
Grafham Water Fishing Lodge
West Perry
Huntingdon
Cambridgeshire
Tel   0480 810531

Draycote
Draycote Water
Kites Hardwick
Rugby
Tel   0788 811107

Bewl Water
The Fishing Lodge
Bewl Water
Wadhurst
Tunbridge Wells
Kent
Tel   0892 890661

Chew Valley Lake
The Fisheries Officer
Bristol Waterworks Company
Woodford Lodge
Chew Stoke
Bristol
Avon
Tel   0272 332339

Wimbleball
The Fishing Lodge
Wimbleball Reservoir
Dulverton
Somerset
Tel   03987 372

Lance Nicholson
Tackle Shop
High Street
Dulverton
Somerset

Wales

Trawsfynydd
The Secretary
Trawsfynydd Management Committee
Prysor Hatchery
Trawsfynydd
Gwynedd
Tel   076687 313

Ireland

Lough Conn
Conn Anglers Association
Mullenmore North
Crossmolina
County Mayo
Ireland
Tel   096 31166

Lough Sheelin
Central Fisheries Board
Mullaghboy
Ballyhedan
Ireland

Index